Reach: Accept and Share

Reaching the Lost for Christ through Social Media

by

Dr. Doug Pray and Dr. Jason Lord

www.TotalPublishingAndMedia.com

Table of Contents

FOREWORD

by Dr. Jason Lord

As people began to shuffle into the 2008 Parker Seminar in Las Vegas, I prepared myself for my first chiropractic tradeshow since launching my business to help chiropractors develop their patient base through social media and Google rankings. As providence would have it, the first hand I shook at that convention was someone who would become a dear friend and have a great influence in my life.

A distinguished-looking man approached my booth. Eager to discuss my exciting proposition, and encouraged by his apparent interest, I introduced myself; "Hello. I'm Dr. Jason Lord."

The man chuckled at my introduction, which I found curious, until he responded, "I'm Dr. Doug Pray... Dr. Lord and Dr. Pray?" It was admittedly funny and we had a good laugh, forgetting all about business. Some indefinable quality immediately put me at ease with Dr. Pray and, upon reflection, it was the deep sense of inner peace that he exuded as a result of living a life that is filled with the presence of the Lord and happiness that comes from knowing that you are doing good work by evangelizing to others. Over the next year and a half, we continued to bump into each other at conventions, sharing lunches and our free time, resulting in many bemused smiles from other conventioneers that Dr. Lord and Dr. Pray were together again.

In July of 2009, we attended a convention together in Chicago. One of my favorite cities, Chicago would come to be forever remembered as the place we reached a turning point in our lives, the first brick on our path to doing the Lord's work. Hailing a cab downtown, we could not have predicted how being put in this particular cab would change our lives, proving to be yet another providential circumstance in our story.

After settling into the cab, we immediately began to notice the symbols of Christianity that adorned the interior, proudly announcing to the world that the man was a Christian, sharing his faith unabashedly with dozens of riders each day in a silent and meaningful manner. The man's pride in his faith was laudable and we naturally became interested in getting to know him.

"What is your name?" Dr. Pray asked the man.

"Amir", the man responded in a thick Arabic accent, confirming that he was, in fact, a first generation immigrant and had not grown up in America, but in the Arabic culture, where Christianity is not only frowned upon, it is forbidden and persecuted. This man had found Jesus, despite the government of his homeland's best efforts to keep him from hearing the Gospel and deny him the opportunity for salvation.

"I'm Dr. Pray and this is Dr. Lord." As the cab slightly veered, he apologized, asking us to repeat our names. As we spoke to him and got to know his story, exchanging some ideas about Christianity, Amir became insistent that "this is from God" and we were put into his cab to "do good things for Christ." In Amir's view, there was no possible way that it was mere coincidence that two men with names like Dr. Lord and Dr. Pray would be put in his cab, believing that it was divine providence. I took mental note of, and chuckled at, his zealous fervor and enthusiasm, which, when turned towards Islam can Prove deadly under the influence of a misguiding leader, but, as a Christian he was the ideal candidate to witness to non-believers, having a true conviction in his belief and passion about the Gospel, enlivened by the Word in a manner that few of us are today. Amir displayed his symbols of Christianity prominently, using them as tools to aid him in his efforts to witness, facing many potential new Christians at work every day and given a personal atmosphere in which to converse with them and teach them about Christ. Amir's fervor to spread the Word inspired me to seek that same dedication in my own life, and strive every day to fulfill the Great Commission.

After a friendly argument over payment, painstakingly persuading Amir to take our money, Dr. Pray and I went on our way discussing the things that Amir had said to us. Was it divine providence? After all, Dr. Pray's had been the very first hand that I shook at my very first convention. We had immediately felt a bond with each other that could not be downplayed to our affable natures. Certainly we were both friendly, but it went far deeper than that. We had been put together by Christ for a reason, but what had we done with his carefully laid plan? It was clear that we needed to find something meaningful to do for Christ, but what?

Dr. Pray made an ambitious proposal, "Why wouldn't your social media and Google strategy that has served the healthcare industry so well work to help struggling churches survive and expand?"

"Like evangelical social media?"

His face was illuminated with excitement as the simplicity, efficacy, and reverberating effects of his idea began to fall into place; "Exactly. Just think, churches could reach their congregation and future congregation members where they spend the majority of their time, stay relevant to young people, and even reach people in Muslim countries where speaking about Christianity to a non-Christian is forbidden... we could help fill the pews again, reach the unreachable..." he trailed off, as though in a state of reverie at his beautiful vision.

That day was a turning point in our lives, the day that we realized the work that we were put here to do: to complement and enrich the church's mission through social media, help to expand congregations, and to spread Christianity and the word of Christ throughout the world. And that's exactly what this book is about; it is but one of many steps that Dr. Pray and I have taken together to help teach churches how to apply internet technology to grow and expand the Christian community locally and globally.

SECTION I

THE WORK

Why is it Important to Spread the Word?

"... and all are justified freely by his grace through the redemption that came by Christ Jesus"

Romans 3:24 NIV

"Nevertheless, death reigned from the time of Adam to the time of Moses, even over those who did not sin by breaking a command, as did Adam, who is a pattern of the one to come.

But the gift is not like the trespass. For if the many died by the trespass of the one man, how much more did God's grace and the gift that came by the grace of the one man, Jesus Christ, overflow to the many! Nor can the gift of God be compared with the result of one man's sin: The judgment followed one sin and brought condemnation, but the gift followed many trespasses and brought justification."

Romans 5:14-16 NIV

We all know that the wages of sin is death. God came to the Earth as Jesus taking upon himself the burden of all of our sins and securing eternal life for us through His death and resurrection. We now have the assurance of a place in heaven with Him. All that we must do is accept His gift of grace and share the Message with others.

Our side of the deal is incredibly simple, yet many of us are failing to spread the good news of grace. Jesus Christ speaks through us and, as Christians, we are commissioned to share the good news of that grace with others; although it has touched us, it is most important that we follow the example of the early disciples and spread the message of

God's grace to others. Give them the opportunity to accept the gift of being with Jesus for eternity in heaven that we have been given and then to continue to share that gift with others. Reach: accept and share.

Bearing Fruit

*"This is to my Father's glory, that you bear much fruit,
showing yourselves to be my disciples."*

John 15:7

It is important as Christians that we bear fruit, showing ourselves to be disciples of Christ by inspiring new disciples of Christ, through exhibiting the fruit of the Spirit of God and witnessing to non-believers God's Word in action. Just as plants are mature when they bear fruit, We are spiritually mature when our lives demonstrate the fruit of the Spirit to inspire others to become Christians.

Rick Warren explicates the concept of spiritual maturity in *The Mark of Maturity*:

> How do you know when a tomato plant is mature? It bears tomatoes. How do you know when an apple tree is mature? It produces apples. How do you know when a human being is physically mature? He or she has the ability to reproduce. How do you know when you are spiritually mature? You spiritually reproduce, or as today's verse says, you "bear much fruit".[1]

There are many methods through which we can bear fruit as Christians; we are bearing fruit whenever we spread Christianity and make disciple of Christ. For years, we have relied on our individual ability to witness and the power of our testimony to reach people with the Word. Though it has basically been the only way to reach people

---

[1] Warren, Rick. *The Mark of Maturity*. June 16, 2011.

in the past, it is limiting and many people have struggled with traditional evangelism, finding it difficult to witness in situations where it is frowned upon or generally uncomfortable. Social media provides Christians with a simple and effective means of evangelizing. And, while it should never be our sole means of spreading the Word, social media offers Christians an easy and contemporary way of reaching out to others. Complemented with more in-depth personal witnessing, it provides a bridge for those who currently struggle with how to share their faith with others. A non-threatening introduction to evangelizing, social media can lead timid believers to pursue other avenues for witnessing in the future. For those with physical limitations, social media evangelism may remain the extent of their ministry throughout their lives, while for others it may provide a new and fulfilling means of sharing that complements their current practices. No matter where you are in your witness, social media can easily become a means to evangelize and can be used by every Christian who has access to the internet.

We Are Debtors

"I am a debtor both to Greeks and to barbarians, both to wise and to unwise. So, as much as is in me, I am ready to preach the gospel to you..."

Romans 1:14,15

P aul considered himself to be a debtor, a person obligated to teach the Gospel and to spread the Word. Just as Paul was a debtor, we, too, are debtors who owe Christ to the world. It is clear that this is what Christ expects of us, but what are we really doing in our daily lives to work towards this goal?

Since our everyday lives already include social media, what could be easier than using social media, in some small way every day, to witness to nonbelievers? Through social media, we are able to reach and touch the entire world, not just our own community and country. Social media expands our ability to witness far beyond what any of us could ever have imagined just a few years ago. Prior to social media, the only option for reaching the unreached was a mission trip, personally taking the Gospel to people in countries that do not have the resources for sharing the Good News, or where it is even illegal to share with non-believers. Not everyone can become a missionary or participate in periodic mission trips. That does not excuse us from the command to spread the Gospel to the entire world. The phenomenon of social media provides an avenue for every Christian to participate in the global mission of reaching the world for Christ.

After all, as David Platt artfully articulated in *Radical: Taking Back Your Faith from the American Dream*:

"Every saved person this side of heaven owes the gospel to every lost person this side of hell. We owe Christ to the world—to the least person and to the greatest person, to the richest person and to the poorest person, to the best person and to the worst person. We are in debt to the nations (74)."

It is necessary that we begin to live our lives each day as though it is absolutely urgent to tell people about Jesus Christ; if we are not living our lives with this sense of urgency to witnessing, then we are not living our lives as Christ commanded. Never before has the Church had a venue for spreading the Word that, with the same endeavor, could reach a soul in Kenya or Nigeria at the same time it is reaching your best friend and neighbor next door. For many people, social media is the easiest way to begin to witness and to begin living in the manner that our lives were intended to be lived. We can share the Gospel with those who do not know Christ and share real answers and information from God's word on everyday life concerns and issues. Every day we can witness with a simple click.

What happens to people who do not hear about Christ?

The very simple answer to this question is that people who do not hear about Christ do not get to spend eternity with Him. What if you could have changed that fate, even for one person? What is holding you back from sharing what would save someone's soul for eternity? If we are not spreading the Word, then we are not doing what Christ commanded us to do and others will not have the opportunity to meet Jesus. It is far too heavy a burden to carry these things in our hearts. We must do our part to offer our fellow man the opportunity to spend an eternity in the grace of our Lord alongside of us.

It is absolutely imperative that we fulfill the debt that we owe Christ, as Paul did, to preach the Word to others. If we are not spreading the Word through every avenue that is available to us, then we are not utilizing the resources God has provided us to accomplish this task. With each new generation, new ideas, new approaches, new strategies evolve to evangelize and grow Christ's church. As civilizations develop and progress, God expects us to use these advances to advance His Kingdom. We are in a new era, the era of social media. Society is using social media for any and every message. It is the fastest, most effective way to communicate information. If we do not use it to spread the Gospel of Christ, we are missing the mark. If we allow our own failure to adapt to modern technology to win out, then we are missing the greatest opportunity to share Christ with others that has ever existed since Christ himself was here on earth. By only spreading the Word from the pulpit or through personal interactions as opportunities present themselves, then we are not evangelizing to the best of our abilities or using all of the resources God is making available to us.

What Is a Life Driven by Commission?

"Go therefore and make disciples of all nations…"

Matthew 28:19 ESV

"What have I done to work towards fulfilling the Great Commission today?" If we are not asking ourselves that question every day, and we cannot answer in some way every time we ask it of ourselves, we are not spending our days fulfilling our purpose in the world and honoring what Christ died for.

Each day, we should ask ourselves:

- What have I done to spread the Word today?
- Have I tried to witness to non-believers today?
- Whose life have I touched with Christ's answers for life's problems today?
- How have I tried to impact people around the world with the Word today?
- Have I done what Christ asked me to do today?
- Who have I helped to spend an eternity with Christ today?

At the end of each day, you will find that it is nearly impossible to provide a sufficient answer to these questions. How, in your everyday life, can you find the time to witness to non-believers, encourage family and friends, share God's simple messages for daily living, and share practical components of living a Christian life and do so in a way that reaches many people? The simple answer to this question is social media.

Although social media is not the only answer and should in no way replace other efforts to evangelize and minister to your congregation and your family and friends, it is one way to do so in this high tech age for people who feel as though their reach is not extending far enough into the world or touching people around the world.

It is doubtful that anyone is going to be converted or saved through a single tweet; however, it is a way of introducing Christ to people, begin a conversation of living a life of faith, establish a relationship, and earn the right to witness to them. Missionary work and the people that we come into contact with on a daily basis remain the integral part of the world wide evangelizing process; however, social media can complement these methods greatly.

Although this sounds like the use of social media should focus on reaching the lost for Christ, as it should, it is also the best avenue to share with the masses the answers for living a daily life of faith. It is the source to share with your community that Christ has the answers for the struggles of everyday life. Messages on prayer, faith, grief, marriage, finances, families, character, and any other life messages you choose to present from God's Word. Social media is a key tool in reaching your local community with your church's personal invitation and information to grow your local congregation.

For everything, absolutely everything, above and below visible and invisible... everything got started in him and finds its purpose in him.

Colossians 1:16

If we are not working towards living lives that are devoted to Him and to spreading the Gospel, we are failing to live a life with Christ's purpose. By beginning to make an effort towards finding purpose, we can begin to live lives that are rich with meaning and the fullness of His blessings. In Rick Warren's *The Purpose-Driven Life*, he makes this point very clear:

"The purpose of your life is far greater than your own personal fulfillment, your peace of mind, or even your happiness. It's

11

far greater than your family, your career, or even your wildest dreams and ambitions. If you want to know why you were place on this planet, you must begin with God. You were born by his purpose and *for* his purpose (11)."

Warren's reminder that this is the purpose that we were born for is powerful, helping us to realize that as Christians, we were born for a reason and with a purpose. Many of us are failing to fulfill this reason and this purpose, allowing our families, careers, ambitions, and personal happiness to take precedence over saving the souls of non-believers and helping them to spend a blissful eternity with Christ.

We were put here to spread His word and His gospel, now it is time that we begin to do so. Social media can help us to fulfill our purpose on Earth and help us to live a *purpose-driven life*.

Why, you do not even know what will happen tomorrow. What is your life? You are a mist that appears for a little while and then vanishes.

James 4:13-14

Fulfilling Romans 12: Using Our Everyday, Ordinary Lives to Spread the Word

So here's what I want you to do, God helping you: Take your everyday, ordinary life - your sleeping, eating, going-to-work, and walking-around life - and place it before God as an offering.

Romans 12:1
The Message

In Francis Chan's *Crazy Love: Overwhelmed by a Relentless God*, he reminds readers, "On the average day, we live caught up in ourselves. On the average day, we don't consider God very much. On the average day, we forget that our life truly is a vapor" (37). It is important for us to remember our own mortality and limitations and that at some point, we will run out of "tomorrows" in which to do things. What happens when we keep putting off the spread of the Word of the Lord until tomorrow and that day never comes? Will we have failed to fulfill our purpose on this Earth? How will we have contributed to the Great Commission? Will people really remember us for the professional accomplishments that we put before God? Will our skewed priorities have been worth it in the end? Will we reach the Eternal Kingdom if we have put it off?

Chan imparts an important lesson on getting caught up with the things that we deem important in our lives, failing to rejoice in the Lord when we become preoccupied with other things; "...there's that perplexing command: '*Rejoice in the Lord always.* I will say it again: Rejoice!' (Phil. 4:4). You'll notice that it doesn't end with '...unless you're doing something extremely important' " (39).

Fulfilling Romans 12 (The Message)

So here's what I want you to do, God helping you: Take your everyday, ordinary life - your sleeping, eating, going-to-work, and walking-around life - and place it before God as an offering. Embracing what God does for you is the best thing you can do for him. Don't become so well-adjusted to your culture that you fit into it without even thinking. Instead, fix your attention on God. You'll be changed from the inside out. Readily recognize what he wants from you, and quickly respond to it. Unlike the culture around you, always dragging you down to its level of immaturity, God brings the best out of you, develops well-formed maturity in you. I'm speaking to you out of deep gratitude for all that God has given me, and especially as I have responsibilities in relation to you. Living then, as every one of you does, in pure grace, it's important that you not misinterpret yourselves as people who are bringing this goodness to God. No, God brings it all to you. The only accurate way to understand ourselves is by what God is and by what he does for us, not by what we are and what we do for him. In this way we are like the various parts of a human body. Each part gets its meaning from the body as a whole, not the other way around. The body we're talking about is Christ's body of chosen people. Each of us finds our meaning and function as a part of his body. But as a chopped-off finger or cut-off toe we wouldn't amount to much, would we? So since we find ourselves fashioned into all these excellently formed and marvelously functioning parts in Christ's body, let's just go ahead and be what we were made to be..."

Romans 12: 1-6

It is important, as Christians, that we become proactive and find a way to become one of the functioning parts of the metaphorical body spoken of in Romans 12. How do we become a part of Christ's body of chosen people? The answer is provided for us within the text of Romans 12; "Take your everyday, ordinary life - your sleeping, eating, going-to-work, and walking-around life - and place it before God as an offering" (1). What could be more ingrained as a part of our everyday, ordinary lives than social media? We spend our days constantly scrolling through our social feeds on our smartphones, updating our Facebook status, and tweeting. Along with spending our time sharing and catching up with friends and family, what if we had an easy and practical way of sharing something that would improve their life from God's Word? We are then able to fulfill this proposition of Romans 12 and work towards the spreading of the Gospel and fulfilling our purpose on Earth.

> *And now, compelled by the Spirit, I am going to Jerusalem, not knowing what will happen to me there. I only know that in every city the Holy Spirit warns me that prison and hardships are facing me. However, I consider my life worth nothing to me; my only aim is to finish the race and complete the task the Lord Jesus has given me—the task of testifying to the good news of God's grace.*
>
> Acts 20: 22-24

Too often, we become caught up not only with the mundane of our own daily lives, taking the children to sports activities, preparing presentations for work, and putting dinner on the table, but we also become caught up with the daily business of the church. We spend our daily lives dedicating ourselves to serving our church, but not to serving God. Though we may spend countless hours helping to plan the next church potluck, charity drive, and doing clerical work in the office, we are not devoting any of our time to spreading the Word. This phenomenon is what David Platt calls a life "devoid of spiritual productivity", in which we are "active in the church but not advancing the kingdom of God", reminding us that "We don't want to come to the end of our days on earth only to realize that we have had little impact on more people going to heaven[2]."

---

[2] Platt, David. *Radical Together: Unleashing the People of God for the Purpose of God.* Colorado Springs: Multnomah Books, 2011.

There are many Christians out there who become too wrapped up with the daily functions of the church to even realize that we are missing out on our greater purpose. Certainly, we are doing good things for our congregation, but what are we doing for the Great Commission? This type of preoccupation with the daily functions of the church can be far more dangerous than the preoccupation with the daily functions of our own lives, as we do not even realize what we are missing. In general, most Christians are aware that they are failing to fulfill their roles on Earth when they are consumed with their own lives, pervaded by guilt and the mental promise to do better tomorrow. When we are already doing good, what reason do we have to promise ourselves that we will do better the next day? It is more dangerous that many of us are not acutely aware of what we are failing to do as Christians, as we are consumed by our many successes as members of our local congregations.

Acts 20 teaches us by the example of Paul, for whom there was a singular purpose in life: spreading the Word to the ends of the earth, that this should be our primary mission in life, prioritized before our daily lives, our careers, and even the good acts that we do within our church that do nothing to spread the Gospel. For Paul, spreading the Gospel was the only reason that he had breath and so it should be for every Christian. No matter how many good deeds we do, we are still not living up to our spiritual duty if we are not sharing God's message with others.

Again, social media has provided us with an excellent tool to offer information for living a Godly life and to witness to non-believers. Through social media, we are able to build personal relationships with others through which we earn the right to witness to them and invite them into our church.

A Global Call

"You will receive power when the Holy Spirit comes on you; and you will be my witnesses in Jerusalem, and in all Judea and Samaria, and to the ends of the earth."

Acts 1:7-8 NIV

This passage from Acts, teaches us that our spiritual reproduction does *begin* within our own family and friends; however, if we are to follow the path that Jesus clearly indicates, we must reach the "ends of the earth" with our words. Being a "witness in Jerusalem", or within our own families and friends, is but the first step; we must also witness in our communities, "Judea", in other cultures, "Samaria", and around the entire world, touching people at the "ends of the earth". By using social media which focuses on family and friends and on our local communities we can consider ourselves globally called to serve Christ, since each social media contact spreads to numerous additional contacts, which spread to numerous contacts and so on. It is as if God specifically developed this information highway to accomplish His goal of reaching the whole world. The effects of this social media phenomenon are reaching the entire world, for example, the fall of several Middle Eastern governments. What better use of this same technology than to spread the Word of God.

In order to be truly spiritually mature and bear the amount of fruit that is necessary to reach all people, we have to find a way to touch people outside of our families, outside of our communities, and even outside of our native countries. The modern era has given us a simple way to exhibit this level of spiritual maturity, allowing us to touch the lives of people around the world and spiritually reproduce with the Word of Christ through social media.

Although the best way to "make disciples of all nations" will always be the path of the missionary, for some of us, this is simply not realistic. Many of us may have struggled with our internal desire to complete a mission and, although social media will never provide us with the same "hands on" experience that mission work performed in nations that need to hear the Word of Christ does, it provides ordinary people who are otherwise incapable of answering that call with a means of doing so in some small way in our daily lives.

SECTION II

THE PROBLEM

The Crisis-Opportunity

"On hearing this, Jesus said, "It is not the healthy who need a doctor, but the sick .... For I have not come to call the righteous, but sinners. "

Matthew 9:12–13 NIV

In the Chinese culture, there is a symbol that originally meant "crisis"; a clear and concise way to communicate in writing when there was imminent danger. Over time, this symbol came to take on a dual meaning, representing both "crisis" and "opportunity". While this may seem counterintuitive, it quite simply means that in every crisis, there is opportunity.

At the end of the day, a crisis is an opportunity to reorganize, make you more effective, and strengthen yourself. The crisis is not a disaster, merely a stimulus for change. The Church must begin to view its declining membership and attendance as an opportunity to make itself more effective.

There are three prongs to crisis: 1. change feels destabilizing, 2. there is a fragmentation of traditional institutions, and 3. there are inadequate resources to deal with the change and the fragmentation. There are changes across western society and cultural fragmentation in western civilization. We are leaning away from the traditional values and focusing on secular, progressive values. The Church currently perceives this as a crisis, and not a crisis-opportunity. The tools that we are currently employing to react to the crisis are resource-intensive and fail to be effective. With the rise of social media and the internet, we can now begin to see this as an opportunity to again establish Christ's relevance in modern society and make the Church stronger than we ever were in the past.

The Crisis

"Therefore, as we have opportunity, let us do good to all people..."

Galatians 6:10 NIV

To understand the crisis-opportunity, it is first necessary to understand the crisis, its underlying reasons, and the long-term ramifications if the crisis is not averted.

- Do you struggle to fill the pews each Sunday?

- Are the faces in your congregation older each year?

- Do you wonder about the future of your congregation?

- Do you wonder about the future of Christianity?

- Do you struggle to get your congregation to evangelize?

- Do you feel as though the people in your congregation are disconnected from each other?

- Do you fail to see the faces of your congregation's high school members return after they go to college?

If you answered "yes" to any or all of these questions, then you are facing the same predicament that pastors across America are currently facing, struggling to get people to attend church, struggling to get your congregation to evangelize, struggling to keep the youth involved, and struggling to get the youth to continue to participate after graduating from high school. Pastors across America are overwhelmingly *struggling.* In every possible way. It leaves many to wonder what the fate of their congregation is, what the fate of Christianity is, and searching for an answer from Christ, wondering why He has not provided the solution. He *has* provided one solution through His gift of technology; however many of us simply are not listening.

We have all heard about Facebook, blogs, and Twitter, if only on CNN and Fox News. Perhaps we believe that these things do not apply to us, are part of the "overshare" generation, or are too confusing to learn. We have been presented with these tools; Christ *wants* us to use them to spread His Word and to lead new disciples to Him, yet we are failing to do so.

If we are meant to use our everyday, ordinary lives to spread the Word, what could be more everyday and ordinary than social media? If we struggle to connect to our congregations and encourage them to carry Christ in their hearts seven days of the week, not just on Sundays, what simpler means could we have been provided? If we struggle to connect with youth, what better way could there be than through the tools for communicating that they access? If we struggle to find people who are willing to hear our testimonies, why are we not utilizing social media as a tool to build relationships through which we can gain the privilege to witness? If we are struggling to get our congregation noticed by potential new parishioners, what better tool do we have than search engine optimization (Top positioning when a person searches the internet for a topic. This will be discussed in greater detail in later chapters.), and social media to help guide people to our flocks?

Today, only 41% of Americans attend church each weekend; broken down by generation, this statistic only becomes more unsettling: 51% of those born before 1946 attend church each week, 41% of those born between 1946 and 1964, 34% of those born between 1965 and 1976, and most troubling of all, only 4% of teenagers have accepted Christ and understand the gospel, even if they do attend church with their parents[3].

---

[3] Rainer, Thom S. *Surprising Insights from the Unchurched and Proven Ways to Reach Them.* Grand Rapids: Zondervan, 2001.

Thom S. Rainer reflects on these shocking statistics in *Surprising Insights from the Unchurched and Proven Ways to Reach Them*; "America is clearly becoming less Christian, less evangelized, and less churched" (33-34). He goes on to illuminate the urgency of the crisis by revealing that less than four percent of the churches in America meet the criteria of being an effective evangelistic church and that for every 85 church members in the United States, only one new person is reached for Christ, reflecting a tragic failure to evangelize and to instill the importance of evangelizing in congregations throughout the nation.

An example of this decline is seen in the Methodist Church which has shown an unsettling decline in membership over the last few decades; at one time, it had the strongest and fast growing membership; compare that to today, with statistics that are deeply troubling: since 1970, the Methodist Church has lost 2.89 million members in the United States, with only 7.8 million Methodist Americans remaining[4]. The average age among Methodists is now 59 years old, an incredibly sobering statistic on the future of Christianity[5].

Today, there are shockingly few people filling our pews. The Methodist denomination is not alone in its shrinking numbers, with Christian denominations across the board suffering comparatively.

In a study conducted by The Pew Forum on Religion & Public Life, only 26.3% of American adults identified themselves as Protestant in the Evangelical Tradition. 10.8% of American adults consider themselves a Baptist in the evangelical tradition, less than 3% identified themselves as a Methodist in the evangelical tradition, 3.4% identified themselves as Pentecostal in the evangelical tradition, and 1.8% identified themselves as Lutheran in the evangelical tradition[6].

Without anyone left to evangelize, how will these numbers ever increase? Will Christianity fade with the older generation, incapable of being sustained by the fewer than four percent of teenagers who have accepted Christ into their lives unconditionally? How can we encourage them to dedicate their lives to Christianity in the future?

---

[4] Smietana, Bob. *The Tennessean.* November 7 2010.
[5] Brown, Rev. Craig S. *Shepherd of the Hills United Methodist Church.* October 24, 2006.
[6] The Pew Forum on Religion and Public Life. *U.S. Religious Landscape Survey.*

How can we stay relevant to those on whom the future of Christianity rests?

Although a myriad of problems are outlined, there is a simple solution to all of them: social media. By engaging in the dialogue around the world through social media, we will begin to make new disciples of Christ, strengthen the faith of those already among our flocks, and become relevant to a new generation.

Reasons Cited for Shrinking Community of Christians

"So too, at the present time there is a remnant chosen by grace."

Romans 11:5 NIV

There are many reasons cited as possible causes for the decline of the Christian community. Among these reasons are: church leadership, failure to foster better disciples of Christ within our existing congregations, budget limitations, cultural fragmentation, and the growth of the Muslim religion. Let us discuss each of these.

Church Leadership

In some cases, there is a failure of church leadership to encourage people to witness to nonbelievers. In Thom Rainer's *Breakout Churches*, he highlights the crucial importance of placing high expectations on the people of congregations. Without high expectations of the congregation, a church does not stand a chance to become one of the legendary "breakout churches".

Although a laser-focus on growing the church is certainly a significant step towards growing our congregations and spreading Christianity, according to Rainer, there must be certain parameters under which people operate. Churches that are experiencing growth have not only high expectations from the members of their congregation, but also allow them freedom to accomplish these goals. Churches that were stagnant and declining typically fit in to one of three different possible dynamics:

1. Placing high expectations on the people of the church, but allowing them little freedom, alienating people with this kind of attitude.
2. Low expectations and low freedom, with church leaders exhibiting little legitimate passion and inspiring very little passion within their congregation.
3. Churches that had low expectations and a great deal of freedom, with church leadership structures that provided no accountability, mission, or vision, giving the people of the congregation very little to structure their lives around or care about.

It is evident that none of these church structures are working, yet churches continue to structure themselves in these manners throughout the country. For these churches to begin to change, it is necessary for someone to call attention to the poor structure of the church and dedicate themselves towards changing the church's format until it is modeled in such a way that it truly inspires the members of the congregation to lead lives that are not only touched by the Word of the Lord, but lives in which they touch others and fulfill the Great Commission.

Rainer, in *Essential Church? Reclaiming a Generation of Dropouts*, goes on to outline the seven sins of dying churches, quite literally seven "deadly" sins:

1. *Doctrine Dilution*

   Churches that are dying fail to establish the absolutes that are found within Scripture, leaving many to feel betrayed when they discover the "gap" between what God teaches and what the church teaches. Diluting the truth as an effort to make Christianity "easier" in order to attract more followers is only harmful in the end.

2. *Loss of Evangelistic Passion*

   Church members learn by example and a failure of the pastor and other church leaders to exhibit evangelistic passion leads to an entire congregation that does not have a passion for evangelism. Being passionate about the Great Commission is the only way to make your congregation passionate about evangelism.

3. *Failure to be Relevant.*

   Churches must adapt their message to fit their surroundings and their times; Rainer expresses this:

   > ....there is nothing more relevant to a lost world than the saving grace of Jesus Christ... The church, however, must find a way to relay this gospel message to the culture around them. The church in a farming community in Indiana should relate differently from the church in a suburb of Vancouver, which should relate differently from the church in the heart of New York City. Churches that do not find ways to become relevant in their respective communities will eventually falter. Churches that keep their internal culture unchanged for fifty years while the world around them goes through continual periods of metamorphosis typically die with that old culture. Churches that ask the question, 'How can we best relate the unchanging gospel to the shifting culture around us?' are one step closer to relevancy and reaching a new generation (17-18).

4. *Few Outwardly Focused Ministries*

   Churches that focus only on study groups and church-wide fellowship events, without the incorporation of outreach in the community tend to fail. These churches are what Rainer calls "country club" churches, excluding the outside world from their closed off inner circle and having an "all about me" attitude. Without reaching into the community, our congregations cannot be expected to grow or thrive.

5. *Conflict over Personal Preferences.*

    Churches that fail tend to micromanage irrelevant issues of the daily functioning of the church, from how to fold the bulletin to the font for the newsletter, neglecting to give an appropriate level of attention to the Gospel and spreading the Word.

6. *The Priority of Comfort.*

    Churches that are stagnating or shrinking are those that stick within their comfort levels, placing their comfort with the way things have always been done within their congregation before the Great Commission.

7. *Biblical Illiteracy.*

    Many churches that are dying are remiss in their theological teaching, resulting in many members of the congregation who do not understand the Scripture, which hampers them as a witness and presents many stumbling blocks to their obedience.

Failure to Foster Better Disciples of Christ Within Our Existing Congregations

Although it is evident that the church's stagnation and decline is a serious problem, we have failed to focus on those Christians that are currently part of our flock. Thomas E. Frank, professor of religious leadership at Wake Forest University, has expressed a concern with the focus on new Christians, rather than focusing on those that we already have; ""I am concerned about a creeping theology that says what's important is to get people into the church." By developing faith within the Christians that we already have and making Christ a vital part of their daily lives, we are making better Disciples of Christ who will be able to make a stronger case for Christianity when they evangelize and are more inclined to do so. Christians who are not absolutely enlivened by their faith do little to grow the community and are less likely to evangelize than those who are enthusiastic and passionate.

Although we may be giving strong sermons, when they leave the physical premises of the church on Sunday, all of their sentiments seem to stay in the building, rather than carrying them out into the world and finding new disciples of Christ. To keep Christ with them throughout the week, it is important that we find a way to reach them in their daily lives, in order to make Christ the focus of each day. By carrying Christ with them throughout the week, the Church plays an integral role in their lives beyond Sunday morning. The single greatest resource that the Church currently has for reaching people in their daily lives is social media. By providing our congregations with meaningful blog posts that enrich their lives and are irrefutable and essential to them, we are touching them in their daily lives, and through Facebook and Twitter we are able to connect with them and communicate with them on a daily basis.

It is absolutely imperative that we find a means of touching our congregations with Christ on a daily basis, yet we are failing to do so. God has given us the means with His gift of technology; why aren't we using it?

Budget

With dwindling congregations, we are left with few to tithe, leaving us strained to pay our ministers, finance buildings, and keep the church functioning. This leaves little money left over to place advertisements in the Yellow Book and the newspaper, and little money to pay for flyers and other distribution materials.

By implementing a strong social media strategy, you can easily overcome the budgetary limitations to good evangelism, taking advantage of the free and far more effective resource that Christ has given us to reach the unreached with His Word. If you decide to hire a professional service to manage your blogs and social media, it not only yields exponentially higher results, but it is also a fractional amount of

what most churches are already paying in advertising costs that have
been set in the budget for decades.

Cultural Fragmentation

The shift in values from faith-based, moral lives towards secular,
progressive consumer-driven values could comprise an entire book and
there are many books already written on the subject. The role that
science has played in skepticism and arguments against religion and
the stories of the Bible is widely known, and there are many wonderful
books written by scientists, professors, theologians, and other thinking,
worldly people, explicating why humans do not need blind faith to
believe in creationism and how science and religion are not mutually
exclusive, that science actually supports the teachings of the Bible.
While we are not going to delve into it here, it is necessary to
acknowledge the role that these factors have played in decreased
church attendance and belief.

Growth of the Muslim Religion

It has been statistically proven that for any culture to maintain
itself for more than 25 years, it must maintain a birth rate of at least
2.11 children per family. A birth rate of less than 1.9 children per
family would take 80 to 100 years to rectify and, historically, no
culture has ever reversed a birth rate of less than 1.9 children per
family.

Although procreation may seem like a simple proposition for
sustaining Christianity, taking a look at the birthrates of Christian
countries is alarming. Particularly in European Union countries, the
birthrates of non-indigenous, non-Christian immigrants are growing at
an alarming rate[7]. In the United States, we are lucky that our large
immigrant population, for the most part, share our Christian faith;
however, many European Union countries have an immigrant

---

[7] Glanfield, Tim. "Britain Second to France in Fertility Rate as Population Keep
Growing." *The Times* August 28, 2009.

population that is primarily composed of Muslims. The birthrate for the United States is 1.6 and, when you add the Latino influx that shares our faith to this number, the birthrate rises to 2.11. In other countries, the numbers are far bleaker and have serious ramifications for the cultural makeup of the world.

Western European Birthrates for Indigenous Population:

France	1.8
England	1.6
Greece	1.3
Italy	1.2
Spain	1.1

Compare the birthrates of the Christian population to the Muslim birthrate, which currently stands at 8.1 children per family, translating to explosive growth within the Muslim religion. Since 1990, 90% of Europe's population growth has been Islamic, either through immigration or birth. At their current rate, France and Germany will be Islamic republics by 2051.

SECTION III

STRATEGIES OLD AND NEW

Although traditional methods the Church has used to acquire new members through "marketing" techniques like handing out flyers, placing an advertisement in the Yellow Pages or the newspaper, and proselytizing on street corners are no longer effective, there are some traditional means of growing Christianity that have been in place for a long time that do still work. Among the things that are still active in keeping the Word of Christ alive are: churches with a lasar-focus on the Great Commission (a purpose-commission driven life), persecution, and prayer.

It is important that we keep some of these principles in mind as we move forward with our effort to grow the Christian faith throughout the world. A focus on praying towards the growth of our congregation and Christianity as a whole and rededicating ourselves towards spreading the Word, we carry out what we have been put on this earth as Christians to do, the fulfillment of the Great Commission.

What Can We Learn from "Breakout Churches"?

"Then the eleven disciples went to Galilee, to the mountain where Jesus had told them to go. When they saw him, they worshiped him; but some doubted. Then Jesus came to them and said, "All authority in heaven and on earth has been given to me. Therefore go and make disciples of all nations, baptizing them in the name of the Father and of the Son and of the Holy Spirit, and teaching them to obey everything I have commanded you. And surely I am with you always, to the very end of the age."

Matthew 28: 16-20

In Thom S. Rainer's *Breakout Churches: Discover How to Make the Leap*, he explores the qualities that breakout churches have in common, attempting to decode the formula for becoming a thriving congregation. While most of these qualities pertain to church leadership, there are many other lessons that we can take away from *Breakout Churches* as individuals and collectively help our congregation to grow. It is noted that the churches that are wildly successful are "Evangelically conservative", passionate about their doctrine and dedicated to living the Scriptures.

We must reevaluate our strategies within church leadership in order to move forward and grow. It is absolutely essential to the continued strength of the Church that we make some changes to the style of leadership we have been using. Rainer cites the vital importance of being open to new to new and fresh ideas from people within our community. By remaining open to fresh ideas, we are able to feed off the passion and ingenuity of others, who may bring an idea to the table that we had not previously considered.

Breakout Churches largely reflects the previously discussed "crisis-opportunity", as many of the churches that are wildly successful today had experienced a period of flailing church attendance, only to find the opportunity within the crisis, become more aware of the need to do something about it, and combine the passion of the leadership and the spiritual needs of the community. This is just what using social media is about, harnessing the collective passion of believers to share the Gospel of Christ with the means to carry out that quest.

It is the laser focus of both church leadership and congregation members on the Great Commission and leading a commission-driven life that make them so successful. Without the leadership of a pastor who is truly passionate and is dedicated to truth-seeking, it is difficult for us to lead commission driven lives and for our congregations to grow.

One of the key factors that we can control as individuals is our own focus on fulfilling the Great Commission and leading commission-driven lives. It is absolutely vital that we model our lives around our dedication to fulfilling our purpose while we walk this earth. Even among devout Christians, this focus often seems to be missing. When you ask a fellow congregation member why they are volunteering at the church Easter egg hunt or pumpkin patch, they almost always respond that it is "something nice to do for the kids" or "something good to do for the community". *NO!* This is *not* the answer that we should be hearing and it is not the answer that we should be giving. The answer *should* invariably be that we are making disciples of Jesus Christ. There is a great failure to be proactive in this quest. There is a disconnection between what we are doing and why we are doing it, inevitably leading to a decline in Christianity.

Churches that show growth, Rainer asserts, are those that hold the members of their congregation to high standards. It is important that pastors remind us of what we are here to do – impart the urgency of spreading the Word – and remind us what will happen to people who have not heard the Gospel. It is also necessary to have personal freedom within those high standards, allowing congregation members to use unique ideas and methods for helping the growth of the congregation and God's kingdom.

Persecution

"...kill us, torture us, condemn us, grind us to dust; your injustice is the proof that we are innocent. Therefore God suffers (allows) that we thus suffer. When you recently condemned a Christian woman to the leno (pimp, i.e. accused her of being a prostitute) rather than to the leo (lion), you made confession that a taint on our purity is considered among us something more terrible than any punishment and any death. Nor does your cruelty, however exquisite, avail you; it is rather a temptation to us. The oftener we are mown down by you, the more in number we grow; the blood of Christians is seed."

Letter from early Church leader, Tertullian, to the Roman governor of the province, published in 197 A.D. in *The Apology*.

M any people over the course of the years have hypothesized that "the blood of Christians" is "the seed of the Church." In Laos, China, Vietnam, Ethiopia, and India, persecution continues to play a large role in the growth of the Church. Around the world, there are places that Christians are not as accepted as they are in North America; in parts of the Middle East, Northern Africa, and Asia, Christians are as rejected, discriminated against, and tortured as they were during the time of the Roman persecution; it is in these places that Christianity is seeing the greatest growth. Although Christianity may not be the primary religion of these places, they are experiencing something that the Christian community in America is not: growth.

While we do not see this age-old method of growing the Church at play in modern America, around the world, it still proves to be an effective means for strengthening the Church. In fact, a video produced by The Voice of the Martyrs featuring Samuel Lamb, the pastor of the largest house church in China, explores the direct and positive correlation between the time that he spends in jail and the growth of his church. Lamb ellaborates that the more time he spends in jail, the more that his church grows, and he is willing to make the sacrifice of spending time in jail in order to increase the strength of the Church in China, stating, "Send me back". Lamb maintains that "Persecution is good for the Church. More persecution, more growth."

In explaining the counterintuitive nature of persecution leading to growth, many believe that it is God's will to make something beautiful come out of something tragic – the touch in influence of unwavering faith on others. When someone is given the choice between denying their faith and torture, and they choose faith, it raises a great deal of curiosity in others about what makes their religion so meaningful to them. In explicating God's will to create meaning in a seemingly senseless tragedy and the power of steadfast faith to touch others, the story of a British missionary in northeast India is often cited. The missionary's spread of Christianity threatened the chief of the village and he retaliated by making a public spectacle out of him and demanding that he renounce Christianity or face execution, to which he sang the familiar song, "I have decided to follow Jesus, I have decided to follow Jesus, I have decided to follow Jesus, no turning back, no turning back." Inevitably, there was no turning back for the man, whose children were shot as a result. The chief warns him that his wife will be next; however, the man continues to sing his song and refuses to renounce Jesus Christ. After his wife was shot, the man is finally threatened with his own life, which, he knows from example is not an idle threat; however, he once again chooses Christ and sings his song. The missionary could never know the profound effect that his devotion to the Lord and refusal to reject Him, even in the face of torture and murder, would have on the people who had witnessed the scene; the entire village, and even the chief of the village who had ordered his execution, converted to Christianity as a result of the man's firm beliefs, bringing something beautiful out of a tragedy[8].

Glenn Penner, in his essay, *Is the Blood of the Martyrs **Really** the Seed of the Church?*, explores why we will most likely never see persecution as a stimulus for growth in the Western world. Penner, a Canadian, cites being frequently asked if persecution will ever come into play in the growth of the church in Canada, to which he invariably responds;

> Why should we be persecuted? In what way is the average Canadian Christian making such a difference for the kingdom of God that he/she warrants being persecuted? In what way does the average Canadian Christian stand out from his/her society in such a way that the offense of the cross that Paul speaks of in Galatians 5:11 is exhibited?

Although in some ways, it is positive that our societies do not condemn Christianity and that we are not forced to suffer through the trials of persecution. This statement by Penner does, however, illuminate the fact that we are not standing out from our society, that we are not making our voices heard in a manner that causes people to take note. It is important for us to begin to stand out from our societies and to ensure that the Word of the Lord is heard from us as often and as loudly as possible.

China makes a strong case for the role that persecution plays in growing the Christian faith, as it is one of the countries where the open practice of Christianity is condemned by their atheistic and autocratic government, yet it is one of the few places in the world where Christianity is experiencing growth[9]. There is an "explosive" growth in Christianity, with a 100-fold increase since 1949.

Today there are an estimated 80 million Chinese Christians. The government only estimates 28.6 million Christians in the country, reluctant to accept the growth of Christianity, despite their best efforts to oppress it. This conservative statistic can also be attributed to the

---

[8] Penner, Glenn. *Is the Blood of the Martyrs **Really** the Seed of the Church?*
[9] Green, Lauren. "Christianity in China." FoxNews.com January 20, 2011.

fact that the majority of Christians in China are reticent to register with the government, fearing the persecution that they experienced in the past. Although things have ostensibly eased, the hostile past is not soon to be forgotten, involving roundups, jailing, and blacklisting. It is estimated that 60 percent of Chinese Christians are attending services in one of the many underground, unregistered house churches.

Although persecution is not the tool by which we are able to grow the Christian community in the United States, let us not forget that our founding fathers left their native countries because of persecution. Because of the freedom we experience to express our faith, we have become complacent.

Prayer

"Don't burn out; keep yourselves fueled and aflame. Be alert servants of the Master, cheerfully expectant. Don't quit in hard times; pray all the harder."

Romans 12: 11-12

We have long been witness that the power of prayer is remarkable and it truly is. When there is a need, God can and does answer it. Although we may often pray for ourselves and our families, how often do we remember to pray for our church and for Christianity throughout the world? By praying for this ourselves and by reminding others in our congregation to do so, the collective call for God's guidance will be heard.

We all have personal examples of God answering prayer through powerful miracles. An example of prayer working miracles is one of a family recently serving God's call in a Middle Eastern country. They had left the country for a sabbatical and, upon return, discovered they had been blacklisted and were forbidden to enter and return to their home in which they had lived for many years. Their lives were established there, their children were in school there, they had all of their worldly possessions there, and it was their home. They were fulfilling this incredible need for people who are willing to spread the Word of Christ in Northern Africa, the Middle East, and other places where the Word is suppressed and a society of nonbelievers exists, desperate for our witnessing. Not only was the family forced out of their own home, this displacement to another country came at a great detriment to their ability to do the work of the Lord, spread the Word, and help others to spend eternity with Christ.

Once you are blacklisted, it is unheard of to be allowed to reenter the country. You are, quite simply, never permitted to return. The missionary community and their families began to pray for their return. They began to spread the prayer request to family and friends through their social media networks. All over the world, people were praying for this family to be allowed to return to their home and to do God's work.

The family continually checked to see if they remained on the list and continued to request prayers on their behalf. After a few short months of living in a neighboring country, the father of this family through faith in God's power, purchased a plane ticket and trusting God's grace, flew back into the country to return to their home and work. For no explicable reason, the family's name was miraculously not on the list and they were allowed to return to the country, where they have now happily resumed their lives and their work. This is just one demonstration of the immense power of prayer. Praying for your church and for those who are working to share Christianity throughout the world is the most powerful yet simplest work you can do to spread the news of Jesus Christ.

Why the Old Ways *Aren't Working*

"There is a time for everything, and a season for every activity under the heavens...."

Ecclesiastes 3:1 NIV

I n *Breakout Churches*, Thom Rainer goes on to explain that it takes twenty people one year of ministering to produce one truly converted believer who has truly accepted Christ into their lives unconditionally. As it stands, there are ten incredibly time and dedication-intensive steps under this 20:1 ratio that few achieve.

The Ten Steps:

1. The Church member must decide to constantly minister, continually watching for anyone who appears downtrodden or in need of the Lord's guidance.

2. The member must educate himself in the Word of God in order to present the Word in a clear and compelling way, as well as be educated in the possible arguments against religion, in order to effectively counter them in a knowledgeable and logical manner.

3. The member must be vigilant.

4. The member must be passionate about his ministry.

5. The member must have the right circumstances in which to evangelize, as it is often not feasible or socially appropriate to

do so in such circumstances as business meetings, social events, etc.

6. The member must have absolute confidence, both in the Church and in himself to effectively spread the Word.

7. The member must be articulate in order to present a compelling case for Christianity.

8. The member must remember to follow up with the person that they have spoken to, as people are not often moved to action by a single conversation, even if it interests them. Life decisions are not made overnight, so keeping the Church and the Word present in their minds is necessary.

9. The member must be undeterred by thwarted efforts and be willing to start over and over again with each new person that they encounter, not discouraged by past failures and not coming to perceive evangelizing as an exercise in futility.

10. The member must be informed and ready with information about their church and its ministries.

Western World Christianity as a whole is facing many major challenges and hurdles to staying relevant and staying strong in the lives of busy people who show decreasing interest in the Church. They must:

- Overcome the traditional 20:1 evangelical resource challenges.
- Overcome world-wide demographics.
- Overcome the progression of secularism.

It is incredibly difficult to evangelize through the methods that past generations have used; although these methods may have worked well in the past, political correctness and secularism have taught society that it is "socially inappropriate" to bring up discussions of religion. There are few people who are open to hearing the Word and finding the people who welcome our witness is incredibly difficult. It seems these days that if you even mention having attended church on Sunday when recounting what you did over the weekend, people immediately become closed off and annoyed with you. It is as if they are threatened you will start a conversation in which they do not want to be involved.

So the question remains, how do you lead busy people with busy lives to church? How do you reach them? How do you overcome these challenges when the Christian community is no longer naturally replenishing itself?

Social media provides us with the opportunity to speak to people about Christ and share real life practical information on living life through Christian principles in a "socially acceptable" and welcomed manner. People *choose* to follow us or to become our friend on social media sites, meaning that if they do not want to hear what we have to say, they will not *choose* to follow us and be updated on things important to us. By *following* us or *"friend-ing"* us, they are opening themselves up to what we have to share, essentially giving us their permission to witness to them. They can receive messages from the Word of God in a non-threatening, non-confronting way and learn daily living strategies from the Word that they might never be willing to give attention to otherwise. Social media is personal, private and permissive. We allow information to reach us and we can take our time pondering it. It is the perfect way to reach out to others daily with God's love and support for living life.

Social media is remarkable in how many unknown followers we acquire, giving us the opportunity to build relationships with and earn the privilege to witness to people who we would have never had the opportunity to connect with in the past. Through social media we build new relationships and we are able to build a solid foundation with the people that we are connected to. Through blogs and search engine optimization, we no longer need to worry about who to deliver our message to and whether or not they want to hear it because the people who find our blogs and websites are those who are searching for information about Christianity and churches in the area.

Although social media will never replace traditional evangelism, it is a great tool to break through the barriers that modern, secular society has built. By beginning to chip through the walls of "political correctness" and "social appropriateness", we are able to overcome the great obstacles that the last few decades have posed to our evangelical efforts and again save souls and build a strong community for Christ.

SECTION IV

THE ANSWER:
AND WHY IT WORKS

Social Media Glossary

Although a glossary typically appears at the end of a book, it is absolutely crucial to understand a few key terms before you can begin to comprehend social media. For some, the following terms and definitions may be a repetition of what you already know, while for others, it may help to demystify the world of social media.

Admin (n): a user who is authorized to make changes to your Facebook page and post status updates, pictures, and links on your behalf. In some cases, this is the pastor and a few trusted volunteers who help maintain your social media, in others, this may be the pastor and the company that you have hired to maintain your social networking.

Add (v): to "add" someone as a friend on Facebook; synonym for verb definition of "friend"

at-mention or @mention (n): when someone uses your username as a handle to mention you on Twitter, notifying you that someone is talking about you; you now receive an e-mail notification when someone mentions you on Twitter using an @mention. If you want someone to know that you are talking about them, simply insert the @ symbol before their Twitter username without a space and follow with a message, or place the @ symbol followed by their username where their name would appear in the sentence.

Ex. See what @pastormike has to say about youth involvement in the church at http://dld.bz/addyU.

Ex 2. David Platt recently tweeted "Grateful to God for @ThomRainer", this tweet is seen by Thom Rainer because his @

handle was included, which is possibly retweeted, to be seen by Thom Rainer's 67,465 followers.

By using the at-mention, you will get that post noticed by another user and they will either act on it or tell their Twitter followers what you had to say.

blog (n): self-published sites with your content published in reverse chronological order, displaying the most recent content first. By utilizing search engine optimization and hyperlinking, you can use your blog to drive viewers to your site and increase your ranking on search engines, such as Google, for associated keywords. Blogging allows viewers to leave comments; however, you can disable comments if you wish.

Comment (n): when someone quite literally comments on a link or picture that you have posted on Facebook or leaves a comment on your blog about a piece that you have published. You can also comment on the pictures, content, and status updates of others.

direct message or DM (n): when someone sends you a message on Twitter that is only seen by you. It is considered "rude" to have a conversation with someone on Twitter, cluttering the news feeds of your followers, so you should use a direct message when you are directly speaking to someone in a way that is not relevant to the rest of your followers. The fast method for sending someone a message is to start an update with the abbreviation "DM" followed by the @ symbol and their user name.

It is a good idea to build your Facebook fan-base and blog viewership by sending new followers a Direct Message that reads "Thank you for following (your church). Please follow us on Facebook at http://(your website address) or visit our blog at http://(your blog site address)."

URL: (Uniform Resource Locator or address of specific website or file on the internet) to your Facebook page and blog can be easily shortened at SocialOomph to fit the 140 character limit. If you are uncomfortable registering for SocialOomph, tinypaste can shorten URLs without registering.

Facebook (n): The world's most popular form of social media. Users go to share their pictures, what they are thinking, what they are doing, and links to favorite articles, YouTube videos, etc. Other users "comment" on or "like" their status updates, links, and photos. It is considered more "personal" than Twitter, LinkedIn, and other forms of social media. Companies and churches are taking an increasingly active part in the worldwide dialogue on these interactive sites.

Facebook ad (n): A paid advertisement run on Facebook that will appear on a user's page when they are on Facebook. Through Facebook ads, you have the opportunity to connect with over 500 million potential viewers. These ads are customized to your target audience by location, age, and interests. You can choose to pay for your ad either when people actually click on your ad and see what it has to say (CPC) or when they view your ad (CPM) with no guarantee that they click to find out more.

fan page (n): a Facebook account for a local business or place; company, organization, or institution; brand or product; artist, band, or public figure; entertainment; cause or community. People can be "fans" of your church as well as being "fans" of your pastor.

follower (n): someone who is "following" your tweets or hearing what you have to say on Twitter

FourSquare (n): a location-based mobile application with which users "check in" to venues

friend:

(n) someone you are connected to on Facebook, because it is more personal, the verbiage reflects that it is someone you consider a friend

(v) to add someone on Facebook, connecting you to that person. After you have been added to someone's network, it appears on their "Wall" that you are now friends and your updates appear in their news feed and vice versa.

hashtag # (n): indicates a trending topic on Twitter, often words that are grouped together without spaces. If desired, you can capitalize the first letter of each word in a phrase to make it more readily understandable without your followers having to guess where the spaces are.

#smallbutpowerful is an example of a trending topic, so you might capitalize this to read #SmallButPowerful if you chose to.

Other hashtags might be abbreviations, #obl was the trending topic for Osama Bin Laden, or they may be a single word like #Miami. (See more on this under "trending topics".)

Hyperlink (n): words that are highlighted in blue on your blog or website to indicate that they are active, taking you to another website or page. Often, hyperlinks are employed in an off-site SEO (Search Engine Optimization) strategy on your blog. As users click through a keyword or keyphrase, you increase your relevance to that word or phrase in the eyes of Google, and such, and will appear higher on the search results when someone searches for that keyword or phrase.

Ex. In an article about youth involvement at your local church:

Youth involvement at a local (your city, state) church has given the community a strong core of service and boosted the morale among area teens.

This is frequently done when composing a word document by highlighting the keyphrase, right-mouse clicking it, and entering the website that you want the phrase to take viewers to in the window that appears. By putting your church's website as the hyperlink, the more that people click this and are taken to your website, the higher that you appear on search engines when people search "Churches in (your city)".

Impressions (n): the numbers of people who have had your status, update, or advertisement appear in their News Feed on Facebook. This is not indicative of how many people "clicked through" the update, just how many people potentially saw it and read it. This statistic is sent to you automatically in your weekly Facebook page update. For a more specific breakdown to see how many people saw each individual status update or link, you can scroll through your profile, while logged in as an administrator, to view the statistics specific to each update.

keyword/ keyphrase (n): a word or phrase that you hyperlink back to your website that you want Google to take note of, or words that you think that people might search for that you include in the basic text of your blog or content on your website so that when Google "crawls" your page, searching for terms that people have entered, your blog or website appears. You may want to include several variations on the same thing, based on how you think people will search for you.

> Ex. You may want to include "Tulsa Oklahoma Church", "churches Tulsa Oklahoma", "Tulsa Oklahoma churches", "Methodist church Tulsa Oklahoma", "Methodist churches Tulsa Oklahoma", "Tulsa Oklahoma Methodist Church", etc.

You should make sure that the terms appear the way that people will search for them, leaving out "in" and other words that people typically do not include in a search engine.

keyword density (n): on any blog post, the title and the first 90 words should be as keyword dense as possible, as well as the conclusion. Your keywords should appear frequently enough to get noticed by

Google, but not so frequently that your page gets punished for over-keywording, or is not readable, which alienates your readers. Having a particular keyword appear about two to four times per four hundred words is a fairly reasonable keyword density. You should avoid using punctuation in your title and in keyphrases, as this is detrimental to your search returns.

like (v): when someone on Facebook "likes" something that you do, giving it the thumbs up, whether it is your church, pastor, a link to a blog post, a status update, pictures, or a video that you post.

LinkedIn (n): a social networking site for business professionals. It is a professional version of Facebook, simply displaying resume' style information like education, work history, career, and a headshot. It takes out the fluff and personal aspects of Facebook; however, it is somewhat limited, as anything more takes it out of the "professional" realm. Having your pastor and higher ranking church officials on LinkedIn may allow them to connect them to local professionals, professionals within your congregation.

mobile app (n): a mobile application for smartphone users. Although there is an "app" for pretty much everything under the sun, from an application to identify a song on the radio through audio, to a business card reader application, to a flashlight application that allows you to use your phone as a flashlight. In social media, this most commonly refers to how people access Facebook, Twitter, and LinkedIn on their phones. The majority of people under 35 check their Facebook, Twitter, and e-mails on their phone before they even get out of bed in the morning and commonly read through their social feeds when they are bored in line at the grocery store, waiting to pick up their children from school, waiting for a meeting to begin, etc. There are some social media sites that are almost entirely based on mobile applications, such as Four Square.

mute (v): to keep a Twitter user from appearing in your Twitter feed. If someone is continually clogging your Twitter feed with what they had for breakfast or what their cat is doing, you can mute them so that useful tweets from other users are more visible. This is a good way to keep following someone without having to hear from or about them all the time. If you have ever wondered how people follow 10,000 users without getting overwhelmed, this is how. This can be done through iPhone and Android or through a web-based external application like Proxlet or Muute. You can set specific users, hashtags, or applications that you do not want to see updates from and for what length of time, whether it is one hour, three days, or forever.

podcast: episodically released digital files that are downloaded through web syndication

privacy settings (n): means to control who can access information about you on your social networking sites. Although privacy has become a concern in recent years, you should not set your tweets to private on Twitter, as it will make it more difficult for you to gain followers and to be re-tweeted. It is a good idea; however, to disable any widgets on your blog that indicate how many times it has been viewed.

profile (n): a page that displays the basic information about a person or organization on Facebook, Twitter, LinkedIn, etc. A profile may give a description of yourself, pictures, background information, location, and other vital statistics.

Qwitter (n): Qwitter is an application that can be used to find out who is "unfollowing" you on Twitter. It is important to maintain a strong base of followers, so this may help you to re-envision your tweets. Having many people stop following you may mean that your tweets are irrelevant, meaningless, or useless, and help you to determine if you are tweeting effectively.

retweet (RT) (n or v): if someone likes what you have to say, they may retweet you, making your tweet available to their base of followers. This is either done through the retweet button or through the abbreviation RT, followed by the @ symbol and your username. If someone noteworthy or someone with a lot of followers retweets you,

you are often able to gain new followers. This was most famously used by Charlie Sheen, who tweeted that Justin Bieber had "#tigerblood". When Justin Bieber retweeted this, Sheen gained hundreds of thousands of new followers. Although it may not happen on such a large scale for ordinary people and the Church, each retweet has the potential to gain new followers. Conversely, when you retweet what someone else has to say, they may begin following you. The retweet button is simple; however, you should always be able to see who has retweeted you and others should be able to see that you have retweeted them. When using the retweet button, it often appears "re-tweeted by @pastormike and others". Who are the others? The only way to guarantee that a person knows is to use the abbreviation RT, followed by the @ symbol and their username and copy and paste their tweet, appearing in their @mentions instead of their retweets. If the tweet goes over 140 characters by doing this, you can always use simple abbreviations to make it fit (if they spelled out "with" change it to "w", etc).

Ex:

RT @pastormike Our prayers are with everyone in the #MiddleEast

RSS (Really Simple Syndication) (n): a way to automatically syndicate content on websites that are frequently updated, benefiting readers who wish to subscribe to favored websites

SEO (n or v): Search Engine Optimization, using keywords and keyphrases to increase your visibility on Google and other search engines and drive viewers to your website

on-page SEO: a strategy that uses your existing website to increase your relevance on search engines through keyword-rich content

off-page SEO: a strategy that employs webpages other than your official website to drive viewers to your website and increase your search engine visibility and relevance

smartphone (n): a mobile phone that offers more advanced abilities and memory than a standard phone. The most common operating systems for smartphones are: Blackberry, iPhone, and Android.

SocialOomph (n): a website that allows you to manage several Twitter profiles from a single page and allows you to schedule automatic updates to your Twitter account. This simplifies maintaining your account and ensures that you tweet at least once a day. You might sit down on Monday and set all of your tweets for the week at once, publishing them at varying times of the day. It also allows you to shorten URLs to fit within the 140 character limit, among other features. It is free; however, you can upgrade to the professional site for a fee, which allows you to send automatic thank you messages to new followers and perform other more advanced functions.

status update (n): an update on Facebook that tells people what you are doing, thinking, etc. You can publish links to your blog or update your congregation on upcoming events. Twitter accounts can be linked to Facebook to automatically update your status; however, this is not a good idea for professional Facebook pages, as it bring the hashtags, @mentions, and other information along with it that is meaningless on Facebook. Since most users update Twitter much more frequently than Facebook, this can clutter the feeds of your friends; however, if you have limited human resources and volunteers, it may simplify their position. Although very few people use MySpace anymore, if you decide to use MySpace, it can be a good idea to update your status this way, as very little effort should be dedicated to a MySpace account.

trending topic (n): a trending topic is a topic on Twitter that is popular and can be about anything, from basketball playoffs to Harry Potter to the Middle East. Commenting on meaningful trending topics may be a good way for you to increase your visibility on Twitter, gain new followers, and get retweeted. The current trending topics are displayed on the right-hand side of the screen when you log in to Twitter.

tweet (n): a post on Twitter comprised of 140 characters or less that is seen in the News Feed of everyone who is following you when they log in

Twitter (n): a social media site that encourages short, fairly frequent (one to five times per day) status updates, called "tweets". Your ideas are conveyed in 140 characters or less, often requiring creativity. Twitter is much less personal than Facebook and other social media sites, encouraging a mass following and a wider audience for your message. While your Facebook fans may be primarily composed of congregation members and their friends and family, your Twitter followers frequently are from far and wide, making little sense as to how they found you or why they are following you. You are heard and seen by More people through Twitter – and the more followers you have, the more you continue to gain. After you hit the 100 mark for followers, new follows flow in daily, as you begin to appear in the "Who to Follow" of others, based on the fact that they follow people who follow you.

TwitLonger (n): a free website that can be linked to your Twitter account to write lengthier tweets when you simply cannot fit what you have to say into 140 characters. This is not intended to replace the Twitter format and requires that users click the link in order to see the full tweet, so the first few words must be compelling enough to encourage people to read on.

unfriend (v): to discontinue being friends with someone on Facebook, frequently blocking them from viewing your profile in the future.

unfollow (v): to stop following someone on Twitter. To have many people unfollow you may be indicative that you tweet too rarely, too frequently, or do not post meaningful enough tweets to encourage people to follow you or care about what you have to say.

URL (n): the unique code that leads a person to a website, article, blog post, or video. In Twitter, URLs must often be shortened to fit the 140 character format through such applications as SocialOomph or tinypaste.

vlogging (v): video blogging; like a blog, but using video content rather than words to convey messages, images, and video. In a visual society, vlogging has become increasingly popular as a means of getting a message across, as people are ten times more likely to watch a video than they are to read a status update or other written message.

wall (n): on your Facebook profile, your wall is the place that all of your status updates, comments, likes, and links appear in reverse chronological order. It is a record of all of your activity and who is interacting with you.

widget (n): an on-screen software tool that can be embedded into your website

Yelp! (n): a social media site that is driven by customer reviews. Customers review on everything from tanning salons, to restaurants, veterinarians, and churches. It may be a good idea to ask several church members to post a review of you to encourage activity and to make you visible to people who are searching for a church to attend. They may post everything from how convenient your service times are, how friendly your pastor is, how active you are in the community, or what your church building décor is like. It is essentially the outside perspective on you and how well you serve your congregation. As web users and consumers increasingly trust other web users and consumers, having positive feedback from "unbiased" sources may help you to improve your image and attract new people to your congregation. You may already be on Yelp! without realizing it, as a business is registered with the first review. Although you cannot stop bad reviews from occurring, you can offset three-star reviews with five-star reviews from trusted people.

YouTube: a place where users go to share and view videos on everything from music videos, a cat playing with iPads, or a motivational speech from your pastor.

Permission-Based Marketing
vs.
Interruption Marketing

"....others will praise God for the obedience that accompanies your confession of the gospel of Christ, and for your generously sharing with them and with everyone else."

2 Corinthians 9:13 NIV

Do you believe the way people access, organize, and share information has undergone a fundamental shift? If you believe that the way that people are accessing, organizing, and sharing information is changing, then why is the Church still applying the old methods of reaching people, rather than adapting to the new methods? Simply put, the Yellow Pages, flyers, and newspaper ads are a thing of the past and are no longer bringing new members to your flock.

At its core, evangelism is marketing. Whether for good or ill, marketing is shaping our planet, and the same techniques that serve modern marketing departments, can be used to serve the Church well. To understand just why social media and search engine optimization are such effective tools for evangelism, it is crucial to understand the difference between interruption marketing and permission-based marketing[10].

Interruption marketing, as its name implies, is something that is intended to interrupt people as they go about their day and persuade them to buy a product, go to a restaurant, or buy a car. It is a sign out

---

[10] Godin, Seth. *Permission Marketing: Turning Strangers Into Friends and Friends Into Customers.* New York: Simon and Schuster, 1999.

of the corner of your eye for a restaurant, which tasks your mind off driving and is intended to distract you and get you to come to that restaurant, whether or not it is lunchtime, whether or not you are hungry, and whether or not you are interested in the cuisine that they are serving. It is a radio ad, interrupting your favorite song, attempting to convince you to Purchase a Ford F-150 pickup truck, whether or not you are interested in driving the toughest pickup around, whether or not you are in the market for a vehicle, and whether or not a Ford F-150 pickup truck fits your lifestyle. Applying this concept to the Church, it is an ad in your local newspaper, interrupting the story you are reading, attempting to persuade you to come to a particular church, whether or not you are interested in attending, whether or not you are even a Christian, and whether or not you are happy with the church that you are currently attending.

These are all scatter-shots, treating every single prospect the same, hoping to hit something, regardless of whether or not the person being hit by your scatter-shot is in the product or service acquisition pipeline. At the end of the day, interruption marketing is an interruption, which is typically more annoying than persuasive to people. Scatter-shot marketing can be incredibly expensive, offering very minimal results. We are currently using interruption-based evangelism, attempting to hit every single person with our message, whether or not they want to receive it and, in this technology driven era, we are receiving the same minimal results response to our message.

Now contrast this with permission-based marketing. Using logic, it is a far more effective use of time and money to spend your marketing dollars only when people are in the membership acquisition pipeline, looking for a church or spiritual support, rather than attempting to spend the money and time that marketing to virtually everyone takes. For example, when someone enters "chiropractors Dallas Texas" as their keywords in a search engine, they are giving all of the chiropractors in Dallas, Texas the permission to market to them and the permission to tell them about the service that they have and how it can fill their needs. Through this method, people searching for your key words are asking for you to "market" to them. Thus, when someone searches for "Church Tulsa Oklahoma", they are asking for information and giving you permission to evangelize to them and attempt to get them to join your congregation. Using permission-based marketing, you are spending money and time to market only to those who want the information that you have to offer.

Churches, whether they realize it or not, have long used permission-based marketing. One of the oldest forms of permission-based marketing is the Yellow Pages; when people opened the Yellow Pages to look for churches, they were giving every church in the area the permission to market to and evangelize to them. Before the advent of the internet, Yellow Pages was one of the most effective means of finding new congregation members, today, the Yellow Pages have been replaced by Google, Yahoo, and Bing.

Think of the various permission and interruption based marketing techniques you have used in the past. Quite frequently, churches ran the same advertisement that they ran in the Yellow Pages in the weekly newspaper; however, the Yellow Pages ad was far more effective than the newspaper ad. The simple reason that more new congregation members were found through the Yellow Pages than the newspaper is that when people searched through the Yellow Pages, they were giving you permission to market to them and they were in the membership-acquisition pipeline. The newspaper ad was merely an interruption, hoping that they would glance over your ad or remember your name. The Return on Investment (ROI) for scattershot or interruption vs permission-based advertisement is significantly lower; the dynamic through which people encounter your advertisement makes a world of difference in its effectiveness.

Any church that does not have a comprehensive strategy to deal with search engines is missing a golden opportunity to use permission-Based marketing to grow their membership. If you believe that information is shared differently today, but you are not sharing information where it will be accessed and passed around, then you are not maximizing your potential to influence people, evangelize, spread Christianity, and grow your congregation. If you are using techniques that were developed during the era of the Dewey Decimal System, then it is time for you to begin looking at new strategies.

The Lessons We Have Learned in Witnessing to Non-Believers

Permission-based marketing aligns itself with the actions of Jesus Christ, who spread his message through friendship and relationships setting forth the model that we should use today when we evangelize to others. As we all know from past experience, by building a relationship with a person, over time, we earn the right to share the Word with them and witness to them, which is, essentially what social media does for the Church, allowing us to enter the lives of the previously unreached as a friend with a solid relationship as a foundation.

Do people really like to be interrupted and handed another pamphlet or presented with another sign or advertisement when they are confronted by Them all of the time: Relationships are difficult, if not impossible, to form through these methods. Scatter-shot interruption marketing techniques establish us as an annoyance, if we really get taken note of at all, to those who we hope will become a part of our future congregation and accept Christ into their lives. By understanding how to reach people through social media, you are able to find common ground with them, establishing yourself as a friend and as a part of their world.

Understanding Search Engine Optimization

".. for the Lord will give you understanding in all things."

2 Timothy 2:7 NIV

There are two types of Search Engine Optimization: on-page SEO, and off-page SEO. An effective strategy to deal with search engines must have both in order to be effective and win the search engine rankings game.

On-page SEO uses your existing resources more effectively, helping you to get the most out of your website. Google likes to see content that is fresh and interesting and relevant by adding page titles, page descriptions, and keyword tags. You must make certain that everything is updated and looking and feeling fresh for Google to take notice of your webpage. Often, churches have websites that were created ten years ago by parishioners and have been infrequently updated since then. The search engines simply pass over sites that have stale content; it is absolutely necessary to have new, fresh content on the site.

Off-page SEO must be congruent and match your on-page SEO, creating many articles all over the internet. By providing contextual links back to your page through such keywords as "church in Albuquerque New Mexico", people click through that link and land on the church's website. The more contextual links that you provide off-page, leading people back to your website, and the more people who click through these links, the higher your primary page is ranked on Google when people search for these keywords.

When you combine the people clicking through on blogs and social media, you are creating a robust strategy to deal with search engine optimization. The market share of Google depends on people getting good, accurate, relevant searches. Google's advertising revenues are directly related to the quality of their searches. You must appear relevant to Google for it to rank you highly.

The challenge is: how do you reach the unreached? You go to where they are and meet them. Invite them to leave Google, Yahoo, Bing, YouTube, wherever they are and join you on your site. Bridge the gap and take them to the church's website or the church's blog site and engage them in a meaningful dialogue about Christ and Christian living.

The best strategy for meeting people in these places is to provide links to your blog, which then provides links to your website, gaining you favor with Google. Although the ultimate goal is to get people to your main website, getting them there directly through Facebook and Twitter does not increase your rankings for future searches with Google.

STEP ONE: MEMBER E-MAIL

The member e-mail shown is to invite parishioners to follow your blog; however, a similar e-mail is effective in getting people to "like" you on Facebook and follow you on Twitter.

Member e-mail

Dear Member,

The Church at Battle Creek in Tulsa Oklahoma has invited you to visit our new blog and to receive regular updates as a subscriber. You can use your favorite social sites like Facebook and Twitter to receive the blog.

Click here to go directly to our "blog" site and choose how you would like to receive the church's blog. www.churchatbattlecreekblog.com
Click here www.facebook.com/pages/The-Church-at-BattleCreek/135332999863159 to like our Facebook page
or click here twitter.com/churchatbc to Follow me on Twitter.
Click here to follow my blog:

If you do not want to receive regular updates simply ignore this email. This invitation will expire in a few days.

Yours in Christ.

STEP TWO: ON-PAGE SEO

STEP THREE: INVITING PEOPLE TO CONNECT TO YOU AND SHARE THROUGH YOUR WEBSITE

STEP FOUR: KEYWORD RICH BLOG WITH RELEVANT, IRREFUTABLE INFORMATION THAT PEOPLE WANT TO SHARE

STEP FIVE: USING TWITTER AND OTHER SOCIAL MEDIA PLATFORMS TO SHARE LINKS TO YOUR BLOGS AND CONNECT

There is a completely different dynamic to evangelizing and sharing information this way than there is to standing on the street corner proselytizing. Using the somewhat conservative Facebook statistics for 50 local friends to every user, the potential for spreading your message is phenomenal. Every 100 church members who follow your blog, give the potential for 5,000 local blog exposures. This number only grows when you are a larger congregation; 500 church members who like you on Facebook or follow you on Twitter translates to 25,000 possible local blog exposures and 1,000 members gives you the potential for 50,000 local blog exposures.

As counter-intuitive as it may be, the cost of traditional advertising actually increases as the size of your audience decreases. At one time local media was the gatekeeper to your potential audience and potential congregation. Now you can take the helm of mass media to reach your audience more cost-effectively. You can take advantage of the reach and depth of social media to spread Christian principles through articles, blog posts, and videos. Social media gives you the power to create an audience and a following unhindered by the middle-man of traditional media.

Social media turns the 20 to 1 ratio that it takes to convert a new member to a 50 to 1 ratio in the church's favor. It creates regular contact coming from the church and the pastor by providing high-quality, compelling content that will get people to click through, whether it is a Video or a blog post on messages such as "Why Families Should Still Worship Together on Sundays".

The blog is the centerpiece of your social media strategy, which is not just about contact, but is driven by compelling articles that encourage people to share. At one time, everyone was told that they needed to have a website to reach people, relying on hope that they could be found. Today, everyone needs a blog to lead people to their website, no longer relying on hope to get them there. Your blog reaches out to people where they are and brings them to your congregation's site.

Today, search engines are the gatekeeper to internet traffic and mass exposure, and SEO is the way to get the gatekeepers to bring viewers to our websites. SEO is the art and science of keeping a website fresh and keyword-rich with contextual links as the most valuable votes that you can have to reference back to your existing website, a highly coordinate symphony to create references to your website all over the internet.

Articles can be about whatever topics your church wants the opportunity to weigh in on, whether it is "Do Parents Still Make a Difference?" or providing information for teen mothers searching the internet while they are deciding whether or not to keep their unborn child. In the latter case, this has powerful implications for the Church, allowing us to nudge our way into conversations and issues that we have been excluded from for years.

Through these posts, your congregation is able to "supercharge" its rating on Google, pulling you to the top of the search engine "found" results. By creating truly compelling content, you lead people to your blog, where, to finish the article, they must click that take them to your website, establishing the critical click sequences necessary to increase your relevance to Google and other search engines.

Why Does Social Media Work?

"Therefore encourage one another and build one another up, just as you are doing."

I Thessalonians 5:11 ESV

If your church membership is in decline, ask yourself whether you are going to fill your pews again by interrupting people who are not interested in your message or if you are going to get them there by having a dynamic, engaging, permission-based conversation. To be effective, you must become relevant, indispensible, and irrefutable.

RELEVANCE

The way in which you communicate with people and evangelize to them must be relevant to their daily lives; the way that people want their information is through Facebook, Twitter, and Google. If you are going to effectively communicate with your existing and future congregation, it is not going to be through a newsletter, it is through tools and mechanisms that are relevant to their daily lives.

BECOMING INDISPENSIBLE

People are bombarded with information and it is often difficult to discern who, how, and what information they want to let into their lives. In the information age, people let in the information that they see as an indispensable part of their lives. Your message needs to enrich their lives so much that they cannot and do not want to imagine their lives without it.

IRREFUTABILITY

When people have indispensible information that comes to them in a relevant form, they begin to see it as irrefutable. People do not share what they believe is incorrect or controversial, so the information must be relevant to the daily lives of the people that they are communicating with. When you share irrefutable truths of life with your friends and followers on social media and blogs, they begin to do your job for you, spreading the Word of Christ.

The way that people share information is through Facebook, Twitter, and their blogs; there is now an extraordinary, extensive, and far-reaching conversation that is going on all over the world. If somebody allows their church or their pastor into their online lives, they become an active participant in the dialogue and the conversation of social media.

Social media literally overthrew the regime in Egypt and it has proven to be the first truly effective means that people in the Middle East have had for destabilizing their governments. The tide of social media and its impact on culture and the world is irreversible. There is an extraordinary conversation going on about every possible topic, all over the world, and the Christian world absolutely has to participate; social media holds extraordinary influence on the culture of tomorrow.

With just one click, instead of going through the previously discussed ten steps to effectively evangelize, parishioners can invite their church and their pastor to meet their friends, family, and colleagues. When somebody invites you into their social circle, it is introducing you to all of their other friends on Facebook, telling their circle that they have so much confidence in you that they are inviting you into the group. Suddenly, you have met 250 new people.

- The average Facebook user has 130 friends after 18 months on Facebook.
- On average, 42 percent of these 130 friends are local.

People develop extraordinary networks to coordinate their lives, even though they may live near each other. Mothers at the local preschool may see each other every day when they are picking their children up, but they are still connected and communicate on Facebook to organize everything from snack mom to play dates.

A Connecticut restaurant owner was running a small, moderately successful Chinese restaurant, until the day that his daughter came home from college and put him on Facebook, forever changing his business. Facebook users are typically friends who share similar lifestyles and interests, so it stands to reason that they would share similar taste in food. After one woman "liked" his restaurant on Facebook, her friends saw that she had liked his restaurant, and also liked it, spreading it to their social circles from there. He began to post lunch specials and pictures, so as the women scrolled through their smartphones, uncertain of what to eat for lunch or dinner, his specials would catch their eye and they would go to his restaurant to eat. His business exploded because he was able to enter a local social circle of people who trusted each other to make high-quality recommendations.

For every person they are connected to on Facebook, they are connected to 130 more people who share similar values and lifestyles at some fundamental level. The same localized power that the Chinese restaurant owner was able to take advantage of is applicable to churches. By being invited into the social circle of their congregation members, they are invited to meet other friends who share similar lifestyles and trust them to make high-quality recommendations on where to attend church. As the friends of your congregation members begin to see their friends "liking" you on Facebook, it will naturally pique their curiosity and interest, wanting to know about you and what gives their friend such great confidence in your message and congregation. We are now able to take Thom Rainer's 20:1 resource-intensive evangelizing ratio and turn it to 50:1 in favor of Christ.

SECTION V

THE APPLICATION: TURNING SOCIAL MEDIA FOLLOWERS INTO CHRIST FOLLOWERS

Using Social Media to Grow Your Congregation

"And he said unto them, Go ye into all the world, and preach the gospel to every creature."

Mark 16:15

W e live in a new era of globalization and, though it may be intimidating at first, this era presents us with limitless possibilities to grow our congregations and preach the word. In the past, people chose their church based on their family's choice in church; however, as fewer and fewer people attend church, there are fewer and fewer generational opportunities to grow our congregations. Others found their chosen church through the Yellow Pages; however, with online databases, our Yellow Pages ads are no longer visible to anyone with internet access.

For years, we have attempted to hand out religious tracts door to door or on street corners with little response, while our congregations flail and experience never increasing numbers. Alternately, some of us get so wrapped up in planning the daily activities of the church that we forget what we were put here to Do: to bring the Word of the Lord to the world. So how do we go about doing that?

Just as past generations adapted to the changing nature of delivering the Word, so must we. Over time, the Word was transformed from stories that were orally passed from generation to generation to written word. From there, we progressively began to spread the word through print, then with radio and television, from radio and television we began to build websites, and, in recent years, the internet has evolved towards spreading the word through blogs and social media. You may have heard of social media, but fail to understand what SEO is, what a hashtag is, and what a blog is. Tweets may appear to be done in a foreign language to you, a mere amalgamation of meaningless handles and hashtags; however, there is a very specific meaning and purpose to each of these symbols. Facebook may seem like a place where people go to share their family pictures and information about themselves, but it is increasingly a place where business is done and the Word of the Lord is shared.

The primary things to focus on are a blog, Facebook, and Twitter; however, FourSquare, LinkedIn, and other popular social media sites and applications do deserve some attention. As Google increasingly returns search results from Twitter feeds, FourSquare locations, and other social media sites, the more present you are, the more that you appear on Google.

For most people, social media is a seemingly insurmountable concept and for many churches, it is very difficult to comprehend how it is applicable to them. An effective social media strategy starts with a world-class blog and many churches simply do not have professional writers with a knowledge of Search Engine Optimization (SEO) at their disposal. The simplest way to implement a social media strategy for your congregation is to hire a professional service that manages your blog, writes professional-quality blog posts, updates your Twitter and Facebook accounts, and keeps abreast of what is new and hot in social media. Although many of us do not want to think of church as a business, without a business strategy, congregations shrink and eventually die. By removing the cost of various forms of ineffective advertising, your social media costs are easily offset. In fact, with a social media service provider your church can join the rest of the e-banking world and have automated tithing a part of your giving ministry.

Blogs

Although many of us may think of blogs as political rants or websites that high school girls go to share the trivialities of their day with their friends, blogs have come a long way since the days when they were essentially online diaries. Today, blogs are the number one way to climb to the top of search engine sites such as Google, Yahoo and Bing.

Although it may not seem important to your church to be at the top of Google, this is how you grow your congregation in modern society. Imagine if every time someone new came to town and searched for "churches in (your town)" they were lead to your church, sitting at the very top of the Google results. Research shows that internet users typically only pay attention to the first page of results and rarely, if ever, make it past the second page. Think about your own internet search habits. If you key in a search request and do not find what you are looking for on the first page, you usually go back and refine your search. You do not keep looking through the pages of results to locate your target. In fact, we tend to believe that the first page of results must be the best results even if that is not accurate. If your church is not pulling top Google rankings, you are invisible to those outside of your congregation.

The best way to reach the top of search engines is to build and maintain a world-class blog. Although you can determine how many blog posts you would like to have, a typical strategy involves flooding the internet with hundreds of articles with various combinations of keywords. For example, you might make posts that include variations of the same words, such as "Baptist Churches in Tulsa", "Tulsa Baptist Churches", and "Tulsa Baptist Church", and so on. You must put yourself in the place of a potential parishioner and what they might search to find you.

SEARCH ENGINE OPTIMIZATION (SEO)

An effective blog takes the skill of professional writers who have a background in SEO to write the blogs in such a way that your keywords are seamlessly integrated into the articles and that appropriate keyword density is used. If your keyword density is too low, you will not appear in searches; alternately, if your keyword density is too high, Google and Yahoo will punish you when they "crawl" your blog for keywords, sending you back to the bottom of the search engines. Although it may seem like the higher the keyword density, the more relevant an article is to a particular search, Google and Yahoo maintain the integrity of the articles that they award high status to by punishing those who are blatantly manipulating the system and are not writing for their readers. An article in which the keyword density is too high is often awkward, difficult to read, and does not flow. Not only are you alienating your chances with the search engines, you are alienating your readers by using the same keyphrase ten times in a 400 word post.

Another effective SEO strategy is using the content of your website to draw readers in by including certain keywords and phrases in your existing website. By simply re-writing your website to include the phrases that your potential parishioners will search for, you are able to use your existing resources more effectively.

All this talk of search engines, optimization, keyword phrases, websites, blogs, etc. is most likely confusing. You may be thinking, "I know all of this is true. I must join this internet era and do it well or we will be left behind in our ability to share, communicate and grow our church. But, we were not called to be computer and internet specialists. We are called to serve others, and care for others." Bear with us. We would not leave you with all of this overwhelming information without helping you with an answer to handling these issues in a way that frees you and allows you to focus on your service and ministries.

TWITTER

Twitter Logo

- There more than 175 million registered Twitter accounts.
- There are 460,000 NEW Twitter accounts opened each day.
- There is an average 140 million tweets sent each day.
- It takes approximately 1 week for 1 billion tweets to be sent out.
- There was an increase of 182% in the number of Twitter users in 2011.

Twitter is mentioned on the news over and over again for a reason: it is where people go to share news stories, interesting facts, and get up to date information on everything from world events to what is going on at their local church. Twitter is often the most elusive of all social media sites because of the special language that is involved in writing an effective tweet.

You may ask: how do I get the word out in 140 characters? Well, perhaps quoting scripture is difficult to do in 140 characters, but it is an ideal forum for sharing links to your blog posts, gaining followers, and sharing what is going on in your congregation. You can use Twitter to share everything from prayers for the Middle East to news of a new pastor, to when your next potluck is being held.

Rick Warren's Twitter Page:

Tweets   Favorites   Following ▾   Followers ▾   Lists ▾

RickWarren Rick Warren

@chadrob Chad, I've never heard of "Chrislam" There's only 1 Gospel, 1 Savior,1 Way to heaven. John 14:6, Eph.2:8-9

10 minutes ago

RickWarren Rick Warren

The touch of Jesus is a transforming power.It heals hurt,forgives guilt,calms fear,inspires hope,reveals purpose.gives life

12 hours ago

RickWarren Rick Warren

Many guys who think they are leaders, arent. Even fools can get a following. A true leader brings out the best in OTHERS.

20 hours ago

RickWarren Rick Warren

Congratulations to the Assemblies of God in Brazil on your Centennial! Praying for you dear friends.

21 hours ago

RickWarren Rick Warren

True leaders create leaders, not merely followers.

21 hours ago

FACEBOOK

- Facebook has over 500 million users worldwide, translating to 1 out of 13 people on earth. Of those 500 million, over half check in every day.
- 48% of the crucial demographic of 18 to 34 years of age check Facebook immediately after waking up; 28% of those check Facebook from the smart phones before they get out of bed.
- The 35 years and over group represents 30% of the entire Facebook user base.
- There are over 206 million Internet users in the United States, more than 71%use Facebook.
- Facebook generates 770 billion page views per month[11].

The first step to maximizing Facebook is to ask the members of your congregation to "Like" your page on Facebook. From there, your word can be spread quickly and effectively. Perhaps your message only typically reaches the 550 people in your congregation. With Facebook, each of the 550 people in your congregation may have 100 to 500 friends, with whom your message gets shared whenever they like one of your status updates links to your blog, or pictures. From there, it can spiral out to the millions of people on Facebook interminably.

---

[11] Burbary, Ken. "Facebook Demographics Revisited—2011 Statistics." *Web Business by Ken Burbary* March 7, 2011.

FOURSQUARE

Foursquare is an emerging social media application that is typically used in marketing for an effective branding strategy. Although branding may not be something that we typically think of with church, the same theory that applies to businesses applies to your church. Foursquare is usually linked to a user's Twitter and Facebook accounts so that every time a user "checks in", it appears in the news feeds of all three of their social media accounts.

In business, Foursquare is used to make the business owner's store seem like the place to shop, be seen, tan, get their hair done, eat, or whatever their business specializes in. When people "check in" to your church, it builds name recognition for your church. Perhaps one of their friends on Foursquare, Twitter, or Facebook are looking for a church and when they see the name of your church appear in their feed every Sunday it builds interest in finding out what your church is all about.

YOUTUBE

We live in an incredibly visual society. People are constantly bombarded with images and they have come to expect compelling video content and imagery as a means of conveying a message. If you have a good picture on Facebook, people are ten times more likely to click to find out more than if you have words; people are ten times more likely than that to click a link to a video, making YouTube videos an incredibly effective way to get noticed.

By building simple videos from pictures and backgrounds, you are able to increase the likelihood of someone viewing your content and receiving the message that you are trying to impart exponentially. You can create these videos yourself or use a company, such as Internet Outreach Solutions (IOS) to build short Christian videos once a week that goes straight to your blog and comes back to Facebook and Twitter. A recent video was a simple display of pictures from vacation Bible school. One mother saw it on Facebook, was intrigued by the video link, clicked it, watched it, and within five minutes of posting, two more children were enrolled in vacation Bible school.

YouTube is a great tool for advertising upcoming events at your church, it is far more effective than traditional advertising and the weekly bulletin. Today, people simply love video content, so by providing them with video content, you catch their eye on social media sites, which compels them to click through and watch your video, ensuring that they hear and pay attention to your message.

YELP! AND OTHER REVIEW SITES

Internet users and consumers increasingly trust other internet users and consumers. They look to other people to help them make informed decisions about where to shop, eat, get their hair done, get their car repaired, and even where to go to church. You cannot stop people from writing negative reviews; however, you can offset them with positive reviews. Three three-star reviews are easily countered with twenty five-star reviews, written by trusted parishioners and volunteers.

Yelp! is the most common review site because it offers more social networking aspects than the other sites; however, the same reviews can be posted to the Yellow Pages website, Yahoo! Locals, Insider Pages, and Google Places. Although people may go *directly* to Yelp!, the other pages are also important because they appear in Google, Yahoo, and Bing searches when people search for your contact information, address, and telephone number.

One of the key things to keep in mind when you are working on expanding your reach through social media is that it can be a slow process when it is in the building stages. It may take you months to reach even 100 followers on Twitter; however, the next hundred may come in a few weeks. The more Twitter followers you have, the more quickly you gain more Twitter followers. When you are using a professional social media strategy, it may be tempting to only sign a six month contract or discontinue the service after a month when you do not immediately have 10,000 followers; however, you should give it at least a year before you can make an appropriate assessment. Even when you have a volunteer maintaining your social networking accounts, you may feel that they would be more effectively using their time in another area of service and quit before you have the chance to be successful. With social networking, consistency and perseverance are the keys to success. You will quickly be able to monitor your success not only in your weekly Facebook page diagnostics and your Twitter followers, re-tweets, and "at-mentions", but also in the number of new congregation members who come to your church. By asking them where they heard about your church, you will quickly discover that their answers are "Twitter", "Facebook", "your Blog", "Google", and "your Website".

Getting Started On Twitter

"Iron sharpens iron. And one man sharpens another."

Proverbs 27:17 ESV

Using Twitter effectively is a skill and someone would even argue that it is an art. You have 140 characters with which to get the message that you need to convey across, and make it compelling enough to encourage people to follow you. At first, Twitter can seem like an incredibly overwhelming and confusing place; however, once you understand it, your potential to reach people with the Word of Christ and touch lives is limitless.

BIOGRAPHY

Twitter is largely based on first impressions and it is crucial that the image you present to people is one that is intriguing enough for them to want to follow you, hear what you have to say, and learn more about you. It starts with a great biography. You have a limited number of characters with which to tell the world who you are, so make it concise and represent as many aspects of who you are in the allotted characters. Rick Warren conveys an extraordinary amount of information in a very limited number of characters.

Rick Warren ✓

@RickWarren I live in the State of Grace
Past forgiven,Purpose for livin',Home in heaven. Loves skeptics. Mentors young leaders. Helps the hurting. Serves pastors. Leads Saddleback. Wrote some books.
http://pastors.com

Others have chosen to create a custom background to provide more information about who they are. Thom Rainer is a great example of this style of biography.

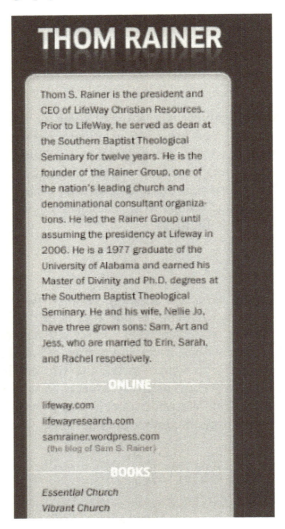

WHO TO FOLLOW

Before you compose your first tweet, you should start by following people. There are many people who follow those that follow them, and many even use "automatic vetting" through SocialOomph and other services, automatically following any new follower. You also begin to appear on more suggested "who to follow" lists based on similar interests; if you follow many of the same people that another user is following, Twitter takes note and suggests that you follow each other.

A good starting point may be following other churches of your denomination who already have a strong social media presence, congregation members who are currently on Twitter, Christian authors, Christian singers, and other notable people who represent your core values. It would be incredibly time-consuming to search out each congregation member from the directory, so begin by searching for those with high-powered jobs or anyone whose jobs may mandate a social media presence. Anyone in your congregation, who is in the corporate world, is a photographer, a writer, or any other kind of job that thrusts them in the public spotlight is probably on Twitter. Begin by searching for CEOs, those with creative jobs, those with jobs in publicity and marketing, and those with jobs in the technology industry.

Let your congregation know that you are now on Twitter. Make announcements, post something in the bulletin each week inviting them to follow you on Twitter, send e-mail invitations to follow you on Twitter, embed links to your Twitter on your website and blog, and embed a link at the end of each e-mail that you send out inviting them to follow you on Twitter. There is no such thing as "over-kill" when it comes to inviting people to follow on you social media, as this is the common practice of every business, publication, and organization that has a social media presence. It is normal and people are accustomed to it, so you do not need to worry about inviting them to follow you too frequently.

As you follow more people, Twitter will begin to suggest people to follow, which will quickly lead you to more people to connect to. Do not worry about following too many people, as you can always use services that "mute" those who are not tweeting things that are relevant to you and are clogging your Twitter feed.

Now that you have a foundation, you are ready to start tweeting.

A Guide to Tweeting

"That is, that we may be mutually encouraged by each other's faith, both yours and mine."

Romans 1:12 ESV

Although you may not see the point of using hashtags, handles, and re-tweeting, if you are not doing so, you are not reaching your maximum potential for followers and having your message heard. Twitter is a reciprocal world: follow someone and they often follow you back, tweet about someone and they often tweet about you, re-tweet someone and they often will begin to re-tweet you. To gain followers, it is absolutely essential that you talk about and re-tweet others.

It is a great temptation to self-promote continuously in Twitter; however, by doing so, you are limiting your followers to those within your congregation and have no chance of increasing your reach. A good rule of thumb to follow is to self-promote in 10 percent of your tweets. You should tweet daily or at least every other day so that people do not forget who you are; however, continuous tweeting is not considered proper Twitter etiquette and will lead people to stop following you.

About 90% of your tweets should be composed of links to news stories, comments on world news, and other universally interesting information. By tweeting universally interesting information, you increase your chances of getting re-tweeted and being seen by the followers of the person who re-tweeted you, increasing your number of followers.

TRENDING TOPICS

People who may not know of your congregation but are searching for a trending topic have a greater likelihood of finding you to re-tweet and follow when you keep up with the topics that are popular on Twitter that day. Trending topics appear on the right-hand side of your screen, letting you know what is trending in your area and giving you the appropriate hashtag for that topic (Osama bin Laden was not a trending topic, but #obl and #osama were).

A good Tweet might read:

"Our #prayers are in #Egypt", followed by a link to a news story on the crisis in Egypt or "#Prayers around the world have been answered #freedom in #MiddleEast #obl #Osama."

Often, trending topics are a string of words, making it difficult to read the phrase. Adding spaces and punctuation will cut off the word, making it impossible to find when people are searching for trending topics. Instead, try capitalizing the first letter of each word, whether or not they would normally be capitalized in a title—include "the", "and", and "or" in the capitalization. Instead of "#purposedrivenlife", try "#PurposeDrivenLife".

RE-TWEETING

Re-tweeting is a way of saying that you endorse what someone has to say, like their message, or comment on it. Although there is a button available for easy re-tweeting, this style should not be used, as it makes it difficult for the person to see who has re-tweeted them. If that same tweet has been re-tweeted by multiple people, Twitter often only tells them "Re-tweeted by @PastorMike and others." Who are the others? Part of the point of re-tweeting is to gain followers, so by keeping someone from knowing who is re-tweeting them, you are limiting your reach. You should instead copy and paste the tweet into the box where you enter your tweets and begin with the abbreviation

"RT" followed by that persons "at-handle", so it will appear in their "at-mentions", rather than their re-tweets.

ThomRainer Thom Rainer
RT @plattdavid: Next @Secret_Church simulcast is Nov. 4, 2011 - "Heaven, Hell, & the End of the World" http://ht.ly/5p89z
24 Jun ☆ Favorite ⇄ Retweet ↩ Reply

If there are too many characters, shorten the words—if they have spelled out "with" shorten to "w", if they have spelled out "Texas", shorten to "TX", etc—until it fits within your allotted characters. If you are unable to do so, use TwitLonger to compose a long tweet.

Example of how you can use a re-tweet to comment on a tweet:

David Platt asking people to pray about a tweet he has re-tweeted from Between Two Worlds.

plattdavid David Platt
Just saw this from Mid East. Pls pray. RT @between2worlds: Christian Brother Missing: Matt Hill, member Capitol Hill...
http://bit.ly/jmOHcP
28 May

AT-MENTIONS

An at-mention is when you mention someone in a tweet, with the "at" symbol @ followed by their user name. This appears to the user, notifying them through Twitter and e-mail that they have been mentioned. Although many new tweeters will begin their message with an at-mention, it typically flows better to incorporate the at-mention into a sentence, just as you would their name. If you would normally say "Congratulations to Joe, Bob, and Dale for completing their Walk to Emmaus", instead say "Congrats to @Joe_B45 @BobSmith @Dale93 for completing their #WalkToEmmaus".

Example of Thom Rainer mentioning Sam Rainer:

CELEBRITIES AND TWITTER

Of course, none of the rules of Twitter apply to celebrities and public figures, who can tweet as often as they desire, with or without hashtags, and about whatever they want, and still garner a massive following. What they have to say is considered generally worthwhile, so no one minds if they tweet often and people are looking for them, with or without their commentary on trending topics.

It can be highly effective to tweet something about a celebrity, because if they re-tweet it, their thousands and sometimes hundreds of thousands of followers are exposed to your name and may start following you as well. These people are often mentioned hundreds of times each day, so do not *expect* them to re-tweet you, as they are inundated with mentions and cannot keep up with all of them. If you're lucky, they may say to your tweet, "like it", and begin following you or re-tweet you. For every time that it has not happened, there are hundreds of examples where it *has* happened. A celebrity following you is a great endorsement for your Twitter page, and you will begin to appear in more of the "Who to Follow" suggestions of people who follow that celebrity.

To increase your likelihood of being re-tweeted or followed by a notable public figure, say something compelling about them that they will want to share with their followers. Like Thom Rainer's new book? Say so. Did you think Rick Warren said something inspirational? Mention it.

You are unlikely to get re-tweeted if your tweet is not compelling:

"Read Breakout Churches by @ThomRainer"

is a boring tweet, which has probably been said thousands of times by many people, and does not warrant a re-tweet.

"Breakout Churches by @ThomRainer is truly inspirational, well-written, and has immensely benefited my congregation. #tourdeforce"

is far more stimulating, gives more specific information, and is more worthy of re-tweeting, increasing your chances of getting noticed. Do not say what everyone else is saying; make your tweet memorable and glowing.

If you are not successful at first, try, try again. When you begin continually appearing in their "at-mention" page, they will naturally become curious about you and investigate further.

LINKS

Your links should never appear as the full URL, as you waste characters and look like a novice tweeter. You should always use a service like SocialOomph or TinyPaste to shorten a link. Simply copy paste the URL into the box, click "Shorten URL", and then copy paste the shortened URL into your tweet.

Here is an example of a shortened URL from David Platt:

 plattdavid David Platt
Praise be to God alone. Thank you for praying. Update on Jonathan (our Global Disciple-Making Pastor): http://ht.ly/5ipUk
15 Jun

URLs can be incredibly long, and some are even so long that they take up your entire tweet, leaving you no room to explain what the link means. The links are often shortened to about 18 characters, making it far easier to comment on the link. Very few people will click a link without knowing what the link is about.

Although Twitter can be a very confusing place at first, when you begin to use it properly, you will be overwhelmed by the response that you get from it. Your message will resound throughout the world and will be viewed by thousands of people.

Getting Started on Facebook

"This is my commandment, that you love one another as I have loved you."

John 15:12-14 ESV

Y ou've created a fan page, now what? Before you start inviting people to visit you on Facebook, make sure that you are prepared. Begin by completing your info, filling in all of your contact details, links to your website and Twitter page, and e-mail address. Write a description and mission statement that defines how you want people to see you, making sure that you say what you need to about yourself, but keeping it short enough that others will read it.

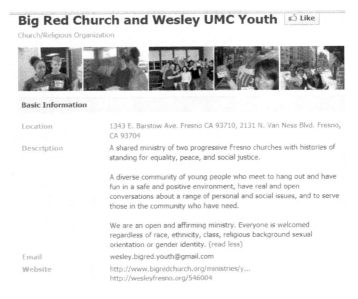

Big Red Church and Wesley UMC Youth 🖒 Like

Church/Religious Organization

Basic Information

Location — 1343 E. Barstow Ave. Fresno CA 93710, 2131 N. Van Ness Blvd. Fresno, CA 93704

Description — A shared ministry of two progressive Fresno churches with histories of standing for equality, peace, and social justice.

A diverse community of young people who meet to hang out and have fun in a safe and positive environment, have real and open conversations about a range of personal and social issues, and to serve those in the community who have need.

We are an open and affirming ministry. Everyone is welcomed regardless of race, ethnicity, class, religious background sexual orientation or gender identity. (read less)

Email — wesley.bigred.youth@gmail.com

Website — http://www.bigredchurch.org/ministries/y... http://wesleyfresno.org/546004

Then start uploading photos to your photo albums, as people will be more likely to stay and explore your page if you provide them with strong visual content. It is imperative when you are including pictures of children to get parental permission to do so.

Serve the Master Golf Tournament 2010
By Christ United Methodist Church (Albums) · Updated about 2 months ago

Stained Glass Windows
By Christ United Methodist Church (Albums) · Updated about 2 months ago

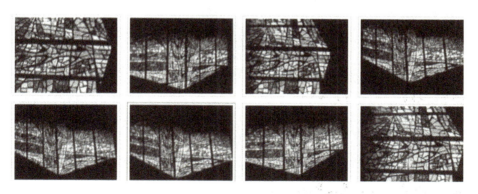

As your profile picture, you might consider selecting a picture of your church, pastor, or logo. You can change your profile picture by hovering over the space where your profile picture appears, selecting "Change Picture" when it appears in the upper right-hand corner, and uploading a photo from your computer.

Profile Pictures
By Christ United Methodist Church (Albums) · Updated about 2 months ago

Invite the people in your congregation to "like" you on Facebook. Like Twitter, you should send out an e-mail, make announcements, include it in the bulletin, and include an invitation to join you on Facebook in each blog post and e-mail that you send out. It is also a good idea to invite your Twitter followers to like you on Facebook. You can manually send out a message or use a service like SocialOomph that will automatically send out a message to each new Twitter follower. Thank them for following you on Twitter and invite them to visit your blog and like you on Facebook, providing a link to each.

Once you have 25 "fans" on Facebook, you are allowed to create a custom URL for your Facebook page. You are not able to change this URL at a later date, so make sure that it is something easy to remember and relatively short. If possible, use the same URL as your website.

From there, continually post meaningful status updates, links to your blog, video content, and pictures. You can either start typing to post a status update or click "Photo" or "Video" to upload a photo or video directly from your computer.

To share a link to a YouTube video or blog post that you have created, you can either click "Link" and copy and paste the URL into the space provided, or simply enter it as your update. You should always say something to explain your link so that people know what they will be watching or reading.

Christ United Methodist Church
A Mother's Inspiration is the video we showed in worship on Mother's Day that touched people's hearts.

Sermons | Christ United Methodist Church
www.cumctulsa.com
Christ United Methodist Church, Tulsa, Oklahoma

May 11 at 8:53am · Share

Christ United Methodist Church
Listen to Bob's Easter Sermon right now!

Sermons | Christ United Methodist Church
www.cumctulsa.com
Christ United Methodist Church, Tulsa, Oklahoma

May 2 at 12:31pm · Share

Christ United Methodist Church
Check out Pastor Bob's latest blog!

Christ United Methodist Church
www.cumctulsa.com
When I was a kid, Easter Sunday was all about eggs and candy! That's what really had my attention then. As I got older I began to understand the details of the Easter story – Jesus' death and resurrection – but I didn't have any understanding about how those details impacted me. But over

The more eye-catching the photos and videos you post, the more likely you are to get people to notice you and find out what you have to say. Although Facebook will tell you how many people have liked or commented on your status or link, you should focus on how many "impressions" each post received, as that is a more accurate measure of how many people viewed it. This will appear below each post when you view your page as an administrator:

176 Impressions · 1.14% Feedback

Although you can act as an administrator whenever you are on your church's or youth ministry's page, you can select to use Facebook as your church on the right-hand side of the screen.

 Use Facebook as **Christ United Methodist**

 Notifications ▼

 Promote with an Ad

 View Insights

 Suggest to Friends

Once you are using Facebook as your church, rather than as an individual, you are able to "like" other people's posts and pictures as the church, rather than as yourself. By "liking" pages that are relevant to your church, you will frequently gain "likes" from others, as social media is largely a reciprocal domain.

When you go to your homepage, the organizations that the church likes will appear in your feed, which will allow you to "share" their updates. For example, Christ United Methodist shared an update from

Leadership Nexus through this capability, announcing that Dr. Pierson will be preaching there on June 5th.

Leadership Nexus

Dr. Pierson will be preaching at Christ United Methodist Church in Tulsa June 5 at 8:00, 9:30, & 10:45. If you have ever attended Christ UMC or know someone who has, be there on June 5! It will be a great time, and Dr. Pierson's sermon is sure to please. We will also celebrate his birthday, which will be just 16 days later. It would be a great celebration to pack the church! Let's make it happen!

May 24 at 8:14am · View Post

As you'll notice in the above example, Christ United Methodist Church appears in blue, hyperlinked back to their page. To do this, when you are posting a status update, simply type the @ symbol, followed by the name of someone you are friends with or a page that you like, and after the first few characters, the desired name will appear. Select it and continue your update as you usually would. This will also notify the person or organization that you have mentioned them.

Your administrators can use the "Suggest to Friends" features to send out a suggestion to all of their friends that they "like" your page. If your pastor or volunteers already have friends on Facebook, this is an easy way to build up the initial foundation of fans.

Each week, Facebook will e-mail your administrators updates on how the page is doing, showing the change from the previous week. This helps you to measure how effective your posts for the week were.

277 monthly active users **41** since last week

76 people like this **2** since last week

1 wall post or comment this week **1** since last week

58 visits this week **67** since last week

If you have multiple pages, such as a youth ministry page, primary congregation page, and page for your pastor, all of the metrics are sent out in a single e-mail, letting you know how each of your pages is doing. You can use Facebook to send out invitations to upcoming events, which allows them to RSVP to the event. This is often far more effective in generating a response than announcing an event or putting it in a bulletin. You should continue to make announcements the traditional way; however, this will almost guarantee a response.

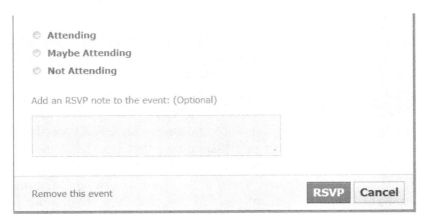

Facebook is a great way for you to keep in contact with your congregation. It is crucial that your youth minister join Facebook as an individual, in order to keep in contact with the younger generation. For them, Facebook is the preferred means of keeping in contact. Many times, when you ask the younger members of your congregation whether or not they received an e-mail, they will look at you quizzically and ask "Did you message me?" Sending a message on Facebook is far more effective than sending a message through e-mail for young people.

These days, Facebook is how people stay in touch with their friends, family, and organizations they belong to. By keeping in touch with your congregation through Facebook, you will be able to procure more responses and build relationships within your Christian community.

Evangelizing Through Social Media

*"I hope in the Lord Jesus to send Timothy to you soon,
so that I too may be cheered by news of you."*

Philippians 2:19 ESV

F amilies are increasingly becoming a part of the social media dialogue together and it seems that these days, a family that tweets together stays together. A recent article in *Wall Street Journal* described the Wilson family that has harnessed the power of social media in a cross-generational effort to achieve tremendous success.

The family publishes a collective nine blogs between the parents and the three children. The father, Fred Wilson attracts 250,000 unique viewers each month to his technology industry blog avc.com and currently has 173,000 followers. As an aspiring photographer, their daughter Jessica has learned the value of social media and her father's ability to tweet about her work to his massive following. Jessica posted her photography portfolio to Tumblr; her father tweeted a link to his legion of followers; within hours, 14,000 of his followers re-tweeted the link from her father, and Jessica instantaneously had 2,100 followers[12].

What has worked so well for the Wilson family is a prime example of the reverberating effects that a single tweet can have. By encouraging church members to integrate evangelizing into their existing social media presence or create a blog and Twitter account specifically for evangelical purposes, the conversation about Jesus

---

[12] Rosman, Katherine. "Eat Your Vegetables, and Don't Forget to Tweet. *The Wall Street Journal*. Thursday, June 16, 2011.

Christ throughout the world will grow exponentially. Although only the most devoted of congregation members will enter the social media world specifically to evangelize or start a blog, as blogs are admittedly a great deal of work to upkeep, it is easy for your congregation members to integrate evangelism into their existing social media dialog.

Many of your congregation members are already an active part of social media and have established social media presences. Although they may have gained their followers for entirely different reasons, by retweeting your articles from time to time, they will be able to evangelize to all of their followers as well as sharing your message and mission as a church. In the story of the Wilson family, the father gained his followers based on his technology industry blog, so tweeting to them about photography would seem irrelevant; however, it was wildly successful. The same can be applied to your congregation's followers; although they may not have gained their following based on religious principles, retweeting your links from time to time can be incredibly effective.

So the question remains: How do you get the members of your congregation to retweet your blog posts? Although you could simply ask them to do so or speak to them about the power of social media in fulfilling the Great Commission, the simplest, most effective way to ensure that your congregation will retweet your blog posts is by tweeting relevant, irrefutable articles that they will be inspired to share with others. The stronger and more meaningful you posts are, the more people in your congregation will be motivated to share your message with their followers. People do not want to share somenting that they do not have strongly held convictions in or they do not believe is worth reading, so it is absolutely crucial that you provide them with strong articles that they will find worthy of sharing. It is through this process that your social media presence will begin to grow. The reverberating effects of a single tweet can be amazing. Imagine if you have 500 people in your congregation, but only 300 of them are on Twitter. If 50 of your 300 congregation members retweeted you to their respective 1,000 followers, and 100 of those people retweeted you to *their* 1,000 followers, your tweet would be seen by 150,300 people. Out of those 150,300 people, if just one of them becomes interested in becoming a follower of Christ, then you have just made significant progress towards fulfilling your purpose on Earth.

More likely than not, the exposure of your tweet will result not only in spreading the Word of Jesus Christ to 150,000 people that you would not have had access to without the retweets of your 300 congregation members, but many of your congregation members will have their Twitter feeds linked to their Facebook status, automatically updating their Facebook status when they tweet. From their Facebook, you will not only gain an additional 150 viewers of your blog post, but you will be able to tap into their local network of people, who will in turn visit your congregation. The interconnectedness and far-reaching nature of social media is profound and it is time that we began to use that power for Christ.

The Giving Potential of Social Media

"Each one must give as he has decided in his heart, not reluctantly or under compulsion, for God loves a cheerful giver."

II Corinthians 9:7 ESV

A lthough the primary way social media increases church revenues is by increasing the size of your congregation, social media makes giving to you missions and ministries incredibly easy. People are not only shopping online, they are giving online.

Both people within your congregation and total strangers are able to give through "giving buttons" on your social media sites. Someone who is not particularly religious, lives outside your congregation, or even lives in another country are capable of giving to your congregation through social media. Although these people may not traditionally be viewed as potential financial contributors to your church, many unlikely people are motivated to give if they like the message of your church or your mission. Perhaps they are moved by stories of what your church is doing for the homeless or the things that the church is doing for the youth. People who are not necessarily religious may believe in your causes and be moved to help support them.

These people were never able to be reached with your message and causes in the past; however, through social media, when someone in your congregation shares something going on to their network, that message may be shared to the people within their network, and you may find that people from far and wide who would have never known about your church or even people who do not know much about Christianity are donating because they want to help support one of your missions and/or ministries.

SECTION VI

WHO WILL I REACH WITH SOCIAL MEDIA?

Using Social Media to Reach Youth

"Don't let anyone look down on you because you are young, but set an example for the believers in speech, in life, in love, in faith and in purity."

I Timothy 4:12 NIV

The positive correlation between youth involvement and congregational growth is astounding; 58 percent of churches that are experiencing growth have cited a high level of youth involvement[13]. For years, churches have puzzled over how to reach youth. In order to grow, replenish itself, and continue to be successful in the future, it is vital for churches to find a way to be dynamic and engaging to youth. There have been several attempts to reach youth, including the "Confession App" for iPhones that the Catholic Church came out with in an attempt to reach youth and renew interest in receiving the sacrament; however, no one seems to have come up with a comprehensive or effective strategy to reach youth.

In Thom and Sam Rainer's *Essential Church? Reclaiming a Generation of Dropouts*, they outline ten of the top reason for discontinuing attending church by church "dropouts":

1. Simply wanted a break from church.
2. Church members seemed judgmental or hypocritical.
3. Moved to college and stopped attending church.
4. Work responsibilities prevented me from attending.
5. Moved too far away from the church to continue attending.

---

[13] Hartford Institute for Religion Research. "Fast Facts."

115

6. Became too busy though still wanted to attend.
7. Didn't feel connected to the people in my church.
8. Disagreed with the church's stance on political or social issues.
9. Chose to spend more time with friends outside the church.
10. Was only going to church to please others.

Although social media is not the answer to all of these reasons, it is a means of combating many of the reasons cited. The biggest way that it does this is by providing a connection to your church, as well as to the people within your church, helping them to feel connected at some basic level. Many of the problems cited relate to time, whether it is in the form of job responsibilities or daily life. By using social media, you are able to reach these people in their daily lives and connect to them in some way, fitting into their time schedule. As your Tweets and links start to become an integral part of their day and they begin to see what you are sharing as indispensible and irrefutable, they will begin to see the Church as an indispensible and irrefutable part of their lives and find the time to come back into the flock. Perhaps by posting links to blog postings related to finding time for Christ in your daily life, and the importance of using your everyday, ordinary life to impact others with Christ, these people will begin to reconsider their stance on the Church.

There is a crisis among "dechurched" Americans who spent their childhood and adolescence in the Church and then stopped attending when they went away to college. The statistics are startling:

Between the ages of eighteen and twenty-two, more than two-thirds of young churchgoing Americans stop attending.

In fact, two-thirds is a conservative estimate, as the actual percentages reveal a much more unsettling truth: 70 percent of American churchgoing Christians choose to dropout of church during these critical four years and few ever return; whereas, only 30 percent choose to continue to attend church. Despite these statistics, only 20 percent of high school Christians consciously intend to drop out of church as soon as they are away from their parents, indicating that there has been a failure on the part of the church to make them feel as though they are a valued part of their ministry or that the church is not only relevant to their lives, but is an essential part of their lives.

Many of them state that they did not feel that attending church was "essential" to their lives[14]. Other statistics indicate that 15 percent of the unchurched youth are the "friendly unchurched", which Ed Stetzer defines as those who "do not view the church as a bunch of hypocrites, and Christians do not get on their nerves[15]" (Lost and Found, 12). That means that at least 15 percent of the unchurched youth are open for discussion, if only we would engage them in it. But how? The conversation would have to be dynamic, relevant, irrefutable, and reach them in their daily lives.

One of the true strengths of social media and blogging is establishing yourself as an essential and irrefutable part of people's lives that they would not want to imagine without. By bringing the "dechurched" of our nation back to the Church that they grew up with and most of them sorely miss, our congregations will grow exponentially and there will be a revitalization of young, fresh ideas and young families within our church, bringing us future generations of Christians.

The simplicity of social media may have eluded some church members, because such a complex problem with serious implications would seem to require a complex solution. Going to where the youth are, meeting them in Facebook, Twitter, and YouTube, the places where they spend the majority of their time, is the simplest answer, yet it is the most effective.

Although the primary purpose of reaching youth through social media is to generate an interest in making attending church an integral part of their lives and spreading the Word, it is also a great counter-balance to all of the negative influences on the internet. Charlie Sheen set a world record for most Twitter followers in the shortest time period, garnering 1 million followers in a single day, thrusting himself

---

[14] Rainer, Thom and Sam Rainer. *Essential Church?: Reclaiming a Generation of Dropouts.* Nashville: B & H Publishing Group, 2008.
[15] Stetzer, Ed, Richie Stanley, and Jason Hayes. *Lost and Found: The Younger Unchurched and the Churches that Reach Them.* Nashville: B & H Publishing Group, 2009.

into the social media spotlight after his notorious departure from *Two and a Half Men*. We are not about to pretend that churches will ever have this kind of overnight popularity or that the youth will stop following the Charlie Sheens, Paris Hiltons, and Kim Kardashians of the world, merely that in their feeds, they will be provided with positive messages and inspiration alongside Charlie's tweets about "tiger blood" and "winning" and Kim's tweets about her new Calvin Klein jeans and partying at Wet Republic in Vegas. No, the Church will not replace the secular, consumer-driven tweeters of the world; however, we can become a part of the conversation and offer a different perspective to remind youth on a daily basis of where true values lie.

Using Social Media to Reach the Unreached

"Go therefore and make disciples of people of all the nations, baptizing them in the name of the Father and of the Son and of the Holy Spirit, teaching them to observe all the things I have commanded you."

Matthew 28:19,20

Although we often wonder what approach to use to reach the unreachable, this age old problem can be resolved through social media. Whether we are trying to reach those who would not typically hear the Word or we are trying to reach those living in tightly controlled societies, social media can give churches access to those who could not otherwise be reached. We have established that the old methods of evangelizing are no longer working. Doing the same thing over and over again expecting a different result clearly does not work. When we try to reach those in closed societies by traditional means, it is not only sometimes ineffectual, but even illegal. Through social media, people who live under the control of their government are given access to God's Word and to information about Christianity with minimal danger of recrimination.

Using Egypt as an example, it is clear that social media is the only efficient and legal means of reaching people with the Word of God and they *can* be reached through these media. The statistics for social media in Egypt is not indicative of the actual number, as many users do not identify their location in order to protect themselves:

Internet	16,636,000
Cell Phones	71,460,000
Facebook	7,354,540 users
Twitter	14,642 users

When the government began its attempts to suppress the 2011 revolution in Egypt, its first action was to block use of Twitter across the country and its second action was to block the use of Facebook, making it clear just how powerful social media is in the Middle East. Twitter and Facebook users were undeterred by government mandates, using mobile and third-party applications like Blackberry for Twitter, UberTwitter, TweetDeck, and HootSuite to access and update their accounts.[16] The 2011 Egyptian revolution made it clear that social media cannot and will not be stopped, despite the best efforts of governments; why not harness this unstoppable force to bring the Word of God to people around the world?

Throughout the oppressed world, social media and the internet is slowly hacking away the power of the government to control the people. The potential for reaching people at this level is enormous, as China, one of the nations that faces the greatest challenges to the open practice of Christianity, has more mobile internet users of any other country.[17].

Facebook provides us with a new method for approaching people. After the crisis in Egypt, an Oklahoma church ran a simple Facebook advertisement that showed a picture of the revolution and asked "We have freedom, now what?" Once users had clicked on the ad they were again offered a choice, asking, "Do you want to learn more or not? Click here." From there, users were directed to a landing page where they could download a copy of *What on Earth am I here for?* and the first seven chapters of Rick Warren's *Purpose Driven Life*, translated into their native language of Arabic.   There were innumerable people touched because of Facebook after the revolution, with that single advertisement garnering almost 17 million impressions, 25,000 visits to the website, and over 2000 "likes" on the Facebook page.

Now, this church has been able to stay in contact with those who "liked" the Facebook page and begin a relationship with them. This

---

[16] Lavrusik, Vadim. "How Users in Egypt are Bypassing Twitter & Facebook Blocks." *Mashable* January 27, 2011.
[17] "Global Mobile Statistics 2011." *mobiThinking* June 2011.

simple introduction through social media inspired many people to hear the Word of the Lord.

Just as the government in Egypt was incapable of stopping the spread of the revolution through social media, oppressive governments the world over will be incapable of stopping the spread of Christianity through social media, all we have to do as a community is to enter and become more active participants in the dialogue that is going on around the world. Although we may not be able to go into the heart of the non-Christian world and reach people, through Facebook, we are given an introduction.

Changing the Nature of Missionary Work

Blog of Brea Persing, a Missionary in Italy

Social media has not only given people access to those who were previously unreachable with the Word, it has also significantly changed the nature of missionary life. Missionaries are now able to keep in constant contact with home through the internet and they are able to touch people at home through their blogs and social media pages, inspiring others to follow in their footsteps and join them in their calling to spread the gospel and witness to non-believers.

By sharing their story, inspirational thoughts, moving biblical passages and books that inspire them, and what they are doing on their mission to spread the Word, they touch many people. Social media is an amazing new facet to the mission trip, adding a great deal of significance and meaning to the missionary's work, doubling their reach by helping them touch those in the country in which they are serving, as well as those at home.

Using Social Media to Reach the Unchurched

"Suppose one of you has a hundred sheep and loses one of them. Doesn't he leave the ninety-nine in the open country and go after the lost sheep until he finds it?"
Luke 15:4 NIV

When we think about reaching those who at one time were a part of a church family but are not attending regularly at this time in their lives, many of us wonder what tools we have at our disposal to lead them back to the flock. Studies reflect that only seven percent of these former churchgoers select a church based on location, meaning that they are choosing where they decide to worship in a different manner. 90 percent of them choose which church they will return to based on the preaching and teachings of that church and 85 percent return to a congregation whose website they have visited before they attend[18], making it crucial that churches have strong internet content available.

Earlier in the book, we discussed permission-based marketing, and this is a prime example of permission-based marketing at work. Those who are interested in returning to church are conducting research on the internet, comparing various churches in the area, before entering the doors of our congregations.

It is important to the continued success of your congregation that you lead these people through *your* doors by leading them to *your* webpage. By having a strong social media strategy, keyword-rich website, and world class blog, you are able to guide these people who are seeking a church home within the community to your congregation.

---

[18] Media Outreach. "The World is Shrinking!" Friday, March 25, 2011.

SECTION VII

SOCIAL MEDIA IN ACTION

A Few Things to Keep in Mind with Social Media

"But I tell you, do not resist an evil person. If anyone slaps you on the right cheek, turn to them the other cheek also."

Matthew 5: 39

With the potential to reach everyone, there are many great opportunities, but also many challenges. Churches need to go into the dialogue of social media with awareness of the fact that by opening themselves up for the world to hear them, they are also opening themselves up for the world to respond. While many of the messages you receive will be uplifting and inspiring, there are many out there who will respond to your message in a negative way.

Not everyone is going to agree with what you have to say all of the time. Trinity Episcopalian Church in Manhattan received some notably unsettling comments after tweeting about their Good Friday service a few years ago, and it is important that you go into social media prepared for this to happen from time to time[19]. We live in the age of *Religulous*, secularism, and dissidents, filled with people who are eager to make their voices loudly heard. After Pope Benedict XVI urged the Roman Catholic clergy to begin participating in social media, the Orlando Diocese, and others, decided to enter the conversation, with limitations. They have disabled the comment functions of Facebook.[20] You too can diminish the amount of negative

---

[19] "Churches Embracing Social Media". *Social Media World* July 6, 2009.
[20] Kunerth, Jeff. "Catholic Church Embraces Social Media—With Limits". *Orland Sentinel* March 11, 2010.

feedback that you receive by blocking the commenting functions of Facebook and your blogs. However, there is no way to control the comment function of Twitter.

Although you are unable to control negative feedback on Twitter, it is not public, like it is on Facebook and blog sites. This limitation of the *social* in social media has advantages and drawbacks; on the one hand, you are unable to receive positive feedback, on the other, you are preventing negative comments from happening.

Before you decide whether or not you should limit the social nature of social media, it is important for you to determine how it would limit positive interaction and how much time you have to devote to limiting negative feedback. If you can afford to pay someone to monitor your social media sites or if you are able to quickly remove the comments yourself, then you should be able to keep your sites relatively free from negative comments. Negative comments *do* occur on Facebook; however, they are less common, where the majority of people that you are connected to are ostensibly your "friends". Although MySpace is the least commonly used social media site these days, it allows the greatest control over what is said, allowing you to approve or reject comments before they are posted.

Many churches do not view this as a problem, and have received warm and nurturing feedback. In a recent *Times-Georgian* interview, Lesa Allison, the communications director for Midway Church in Villa Rica, Georgia communicated what a positive medium it has been for members of the congregation to interact, share prayer requests, and make comments. Despite the churches that have cited reticence to allow commenting, Midway Church has been on social media for over a year and has found the two-way dialogue to be overwhelmingly positive; "It's a great way to get your message across and it's a very positive avenue to get the message out there."

Brian Dodd, a church stewardship and leadership consultant, reminds pastors and churches that although social media gives you the power to create "tribes", there is a "gestation period to the Tribe", taking time and patience to build[21]. Another important consideration is the necessity of obtaining parental permission before posting pictures of children to any of your social media sites. Social media does many wonderful things for enriching your ministry and its evangelism process; however, you must take into account that there are special considerations that come along with it.

---

[21] Dodd, Brian. "What Churches Should Learn from Social Media and the Egyptian Revolution". *Brian Dodd on Leadership: helping Create a Soundtrack to the Lives of Leaders* January 29, 2011.

Churches Using Social Media to Connect with Busy People

"But Martha was distracted by all the preparations that had to be made..."Martha, Martha", the Lord answered "You are worried and upset about many things, but few things are needed-or indeed only one. Mary has chosen what is better and it will not be taken away from her"

Luke 10:40, 41-42 NIV

L ifeWay Research conducted a recent study of 1,003 Protestant congregations in September of 2010 through Fellowship Technologies, their digital partner, showing that 78 percent of churches today currently maintain websites, compared to only eight percent in a similar study conducted in 2006. Of the social media sites that churches used in this study, Facebook was by far the most popular, with 47 percent of churches currently participating on Facebook[22].

Pat Reynolds, a church administrator at First United Methodist Church in Carrollton, Georgia cited the value of using Facebook to reach out to the youth in a recent interview with *Times-Georgian*; "Social media has become a more popular and accessible way to reach people in a timely manner... It's used widely through our youth program. We want to reach as many people as we possibly can to share the Word." Rev. Katie Mattox, an Associate Pastor at First United Methodist reflects the comments of Reynolds, illuminating the

---

[22] Thomas, Amanda. "Churches Extending their Reach through Social Media." *Times-Georgian.* June 19 2011.

ability that social media gives them to translate the Word to the modern day; "It gives us more potential to reach people and speak the more current language of the people... The gospel of Jesus Christ is infinitely translatable into any language or media that is available to us. We should take the opportunity to use it so we can reach people who are using those media."

Lesa Allison, communications director of Midway Church in Villa Rica, Georgia, has found that Twitter and Facebook are extraordinary tools for the church to use to keep in touch with busy people who have busy lives; "We just noticed that people are busy sometimes. They have a lot of clutter in their lives so we try to get a concise message out to them that doesn't clutter up but keeps them informed." Other churches have noted the same accessibility to busy congregation members, noting that people who are following their Twitter page are able to receive immediate updates on their mobile phones and both Twitter and Facebook have been an excellent means of distributing information and announcements quickly.

Other churches have found that Facebook has been the single greatest thing to happen to their youth programs; Jamey Winters, student and worship pastor at North Point Baptist Church in Carrollton, Georgia, told the *Times-Georgian* that before the church started using social media, it was often difficult to get a response from the youth about upcoming events; "For many teens, all they know is Facebook... I could call them and e-mail them and not get a response. I started using Facebook—immediate responses... it became a much quicker way for us to contact them." He goes on to explain that people often look for the same thing in churches that they do in businesses, expecting them to keep everything up to date, asking "Why should we expect them to come to a place of worship with anything less?"

Brian Dodd, in his article, *"What Churches Should Learn from Social Media and the Egyptian Revolution"* cited many benefits to social media and highlighted many crucial aspects of a church's social media strategy. In suggesting that the pastor post updates to their blog at least three to four times a week, he highlighted the personal relationship that this provides, bridging otherwise un-crossable time constraints; "You can't have breakfast or lunch with everyone in your church. However, you have the ability to connect with people where they are, tell them what you are thinking and feeling, and solicit feedback.

These are just a few examples of churches that have cited strong benefits from implementing a social media strategy. Although there are churches all over the nation that have found their way into the conversation, there are many that are not yet a part of that conversation. Whether you are struggling with your youth ministry or simply having trouble getting your congregation to read the bulletin, there are a myriad of benefits to entering the world of blogging, Twitter and Facebook.

Making Church an Essential Part
of People's Lives

"And we exhort you, brethren, admonish the idlers, encourage the fainthearted, help the weak, be patient with them all."

I Thessalonians 5:14

C hurch should be an essential part of people's daily lives. To paraphrase Leonard Sweet, church is something that should be experienced, not something to be "gone to" on Sunday mornings[23]. Christianity needs community to thrive, not just "religious convictions confirmed from the pulpit" (Sweet, 132). The question remains: we struggle enough to get people to church every Sunday, how do we become a part of people's daily lives, not just their weekly lives?

The simple answer to this question is utilizing social media and the creation of meaningful, life-enriching blog posts. Social media touches people's lives every day in which the church simply did not have the resources to do in the past. Now that God has given us the gift of technology, we need to use it to bring the church into people's lives every day.

Our congregation members lead incredibly busy lives, so expecting them to have the time to engage not only in Sunday services, but also Bible study groups, fellowships, and other church groups on a daily or even a regular basis is simply unrealistic. People check their Facebook and Twitter pages multiple times each day, both from their computer and on their phones, waiting in line at the grocery store or waiting for

---

[23] Sweet, Leonard. *The Gospel According to Starbucks: Living with a Grande Passion.* Colorado Springs: Waterbrook Multnomah Press, 2007.

their children's soccer practice to be over. Social media *is* a part of people's daily lives. Through social media, the Church can be a part of people's daily lives. Now, church can be experienced, rather than "gone to."

To address the second prong of Sweet's statement on churches, that they need community to thrive, social media provides us with an engaging new way to do this. In the past, people often missed our efforts at building community, either too busy to go, to disconnected from other church members, or viewing it as more of an obligation than a privilege.

Through social media, we are able to build strong ties between our churches and our congregation members. As we learned from Rainer, one of the top reasons for a person becoming dechurched was a lack of feeling connected to the church and the other members of their congregation. By building a thriving, inter-connected virtual community, we are able to build a thriving, inter-connected community within our congregation. Through blogs, Facebook, and Twitter, what the pastor has to say becomes a meaningful part of people's lives that they do not want to imagine their lives without and through community interaction on these sites and posts, the other members of the community become unified in Christ. Just as the church becomes a meaningful part of their lives, so do the other members of the congregation. Social media allows like-minded individuals to come together to have a conversation about Christ, building a bond within our communities.

It is an incredibly powerful tool that we have been provided with, answering many of the questions and solving many of the problems that have eluded us for decades. Social media can change the entire vibe of your congregation and bring people closer together in a manner that is absolutely remarkable.

We are taught in Thessalonians that community is an absolutely vital component of faith. By surrounding the idlers, the fainthearted, and the weak with the love and support of other Christians, they are nourished by their faith and given a helping hand to support them and guide them on their journey. Left alone, the idlers, fainthearted, and weak are left to their own devices to justify their laziness[24] or to become paralyzed by their weaknesses.

---

[24] McLaughlin, Craig. "Daily Scripture Meditations: Community". *Pastor's Blog* March 6, 2009.

Why Do You Need a Social Media Strategy?

"Thanks be to God for his indescribable gift!"

2 Corinthians 9:15

A lthough this book has presented you with a myriad of benefits throughout its pages, summing up the key benefits will help you to make sense of what you have read, how it applies to Christianity, and how it applies to your congregation.

The Universal Benefits:

- Social media helps us to fulfill the Great Commission and do what Christ has asked us to do.
- Social media helps us to build relationships with people to earn the right to witness to them.
- Social media helps us to reach the unreachable.
- Social media helps us to evangelize in countries where speaking about Christianity openly is prohibited. It allows us to go into the heart of the non-Christian world without ever stepping foot outside of our own town.

The Benefits to Your Congregation:

- Any church that is ignoring social media is making itself irrelevant and ineffective.
- Social media allows you to control your message. In the case of review sites, someone out there is already saying something

about your church, and being able to engage in the conversation and respond is a powerful and necessary tool.

- Social media allows you to reach busy people.
- Social media allows you to reach your congregation on a daily basis and become an ever-present part of their lives.
- Social media helps you to reach the youth within your congregation more effectively. By helping your youth program to grow, you are helping your church to grow and ensuring future generations' faithfulness to the Church.
- Social media helps you to increase the size of your congregation through permission-based outreach techniques.
- Social media helps you to stay connected to your missionaries.
- Social media allows you to evangelize and increase the size of your congregation in a budget-effective manner, replacing your Yellow Book ad, newspaper ad, printing costs, and any other less effective marketing techniques that you are employing.
- You are able to replace resource-intensive evangelizing with a very simple means of evangelizing. This encourages those in your congregation who are not doing as much as they should or could to witness to begin to do so in a non-threatening, non-imposing manner. Although it will never completely replace traditional evangelizing, it is an excellent method of getting more people to participate.
- There is a great giving potential to social media, it provides increased giving opportunities and new ways to give through e-banking. It also reaches people who might not otherwise know about you or your message and, upon hearing it, wish to support it financially.
- Blogs are an efficient method of increasing your relevance, irrefutability, and indispensability.
- Social media helps people to find you and find out what your congregation is about.
- Social media has a pyramid-like effect, allowing you to use the social media presences that your congregation already has in

place to spread throughout the world exponentially to be viewed by hundreds of thousands of people.

- Social media helps the people in your congregation to feel more connected to both the pastor and to each other. This not only increases the sense of unity throughout your church, but exudes a harmonious and inviting vibe to people who are "shopping" your church. The interconnectedness does wonders for your congregation retention, keeping people in your church, as people who do not feel connected often seek out a new church or stop going altogether. Feeling disconnected from the rest of the congregation is one of the top reasons cited for becoming dechurched.

These are only a few of the many benefits of developing a social media strategy, and each church, youth minister, pastor, and Christian inevitably develops their own stories about how social media has touched their lives, enhanced their evangelism, and helped them to grow and prosper. The potential to implementing and using social media for Christ is limitless, both to your congregation and to Christianity as a whole, so why aren't we all utilizing God's gift of technology?

Overwhelmed?

If you, like many people are completely overwhelmed by the world of social media, there *is* a solution. Perhaps you see the value of social media, the things it can do for your congregation, and the things that it can do for Christianity, but remain completely eluded by the process. You are reading this book and thinking, "This can't be done; *I* don't know how to do this, no one in my congregation is skilled enough with writing nor do they have the time to write keyword rich blog posts, optimize our web content, and implement a social media strategy."

For many people, the best answer is to hire a company that specializes in social media and internet marketing. While there are many companies that provide these services, few people understand how to do it effectively for churches, understand the needs of the Church, and understand and have the complete conviction in the Word that is necessary to do the job well.

Internet Outreach Solutions (IOS) is a company that specializes in search engine optimization, Twitter, Facebook, and YouTube video content exclusively for churches. They create your blog posts and your YouTube videos for you and maintain your Twitter and Facebook accounts. Through them, you are able to utilize God's gift of technology, whether or not you understand it.

Many people shy away from social media and search engine optimization because they simply find it too confusing or too difficult to learn. Many pastors have held their positions for years, before social media, Google, Yahoo, or the internet ever came to be and simply cannot fathom using it effectively. By visiting www.internetoutreachsolutions.com, you are able to use the simple "check the box" system, which involves merely checking the box that you are ready to evangelize in a new way, reach new people, and grow your congregation, a system that is easy enough for anyone from every generation to understand. Although social media is knowledge and time intensive, you are able to relieve yourself of the burden of social media, blogging, and producing video content, while still taking advantage of the gift that God has provided us in technology.

Writing for search engines is vastly different than writing for general educational or entertainment purposes, particularly when you are trying to cast a wider net. Enlisting the help of professionals, rather than leaving pastors at the mercy of their own ability and understanding of the SEO process may be crucial. IOS interconnects the blog posts to your congregation's social media pages, making it accessible to your congregation in whichever source of media they prefer. If someone is an avid Facebook user, they can access it that way; if they are an avid Twitter user, they can access it there. IOS unfailingly gets churches to the first page of Google for keyword search results.

Once we start having permission-based conversations and reach people in the places that they already are, we can become a crucial part of the dialogue on every topic that we are interested in being involved in and lead people to Christ. The outreach opportunity for churches to reach their community for Christ and reach the world for Christ simultaneously is astounding. The ability for the local church to operate in the high tech, e-commerce world of today, to serve their parishioners with on-demand access and giving opportunities, will keep the Church relevant and indispensible in their lives. The application of search engine optimization and social media to the Church is, quite simply, the largest and most effective outreach offensive devised in human history.

CONCLUSION

It is important that we as Christians begin to utilize God's gift of technology and start using it to glorify Him, rather than simply using it to better our own lives. It is crucial that each and every one of us approach each day with an aim to share the Word of the Lord as though it is absolutely urgent, to integrate it into our everyday, ordinary lives and fulfill Christ's message in Romans 12.

Perhaps you think that mission work and other means of spreading the Word are simply not realistic for you. This does not mean that you cannot participate in the evangelical process. Social media provides ordinary Christians with the power to do something extraordinary, touching lives around the world. The power of social media is tremendous and by simply using it to do good and to spread His Word, the Church is able to enter the worldwide dialogue with a message of hope and salvation.

In order for the Church to survive and grow, each church will have to dedicate itself to becoming a part of this extraordinary dialogue and each Christian will have to dedicate themselves. Yes, social media is a huge step towards beginning to fill our pews once again and to grow, possibly allowing us to become one of the "breakout churches" of the nation; however, the potential of social media goes far deeper than that, allowing us to evangelize around the world, to witness to nonbelievers the world over and to truly fulfill the mandate from God; He did not limit our role as a witness to "Jerusalem", which in the modern day is our community, He intends for each person to witness to everyone that they come into contact with, as well as seeking out contact around the world.

Through social media, we are able to spread the Word to places where even speaking about Christianity is illegal and to save the nonbelievers of other nations from governments whose autocratic rule would keep them from spending an eternity with Christ. Within our own community, we are able to establish relationships with people that give us the privilege to witness to them, growing the Church within our own congregations and our own community.

By making this simple change within your everyday, ordinary life, the effects within your congregation and around the world will be profound. Fulfilling the Great Commission is just a click away, so it is time that we start taking action and fulfilling our commission in life.

PROLOGUE

by Dr. Doug Pray

When I met Dr. Jason Lord in 2008, I immediately sensed something exceptional about him. He comes across as a kind of boy wonder... always one step ahead of everyone else, remarkably creative, and someone who instinctively understands how to reach people with a message and to grow a business. Although I would have never considered the idea of using social media to evangelize before meeting Dr. Lord, after seeing how successfully it could be applied to the business world, I became convinced that a social media strategy is exactly what the Church needs.

We are facing a great crisis within the Church right now as our congregation sizes flail, the average age gets increasingly older each year, and it seems that our effort to share Christianity only reaches a few of the younger generation. By harnessing the extraordinary power of something that has worked so well in the business world, we can use the social networking of our existing church members to grow our own local congregation and, in fact, share the good news of Jesus Christ with hundreds of thousands, if not millions of souls through the social networks we are already using every day. There is an extraordinary dialogue going on around the world on every possible topic and it is absolutely necessary that the Church enter that discussion and become a contributor.

We know as Christians that we are to share the story of Christ with nonbelievers. In this changing world we find ourselves struggling with how to accomplish that commission (Matthew 28:19-20). Dr. Lord and I have already witnessed churches experiencing tremendous success in congregational growth and outreach by implementing Internet Outreach Solutions (IOS) social media strategy. This may be a new concept for you; to use social media to reach the world for Christ. We want to share the system and techniques that have already been victorious for churches to help ensure the success of using social media to reach your community. You are very aware that social media is the avenue that all businesses and organizations must move toward for growth. That includes churches. For all of the pastors struggling to fill their pews and who are worried over how to develop and implement a successful outreach program, we hope we have eased your mind by offering you a solution that will make social media outreach an answer to your growth and outreach concerns rather than another problem you must add to your list of duties. Through this book, Dr. Lord and I hope to help you turn your congregation's followers on social media networks into followers of Christ.

As Christians, we all know how important relationships can be. Our relationship with Christ gives meaning to our life; our relationships within the Church not only provide us with lifelong and meaningful friendships with like-minded people, but also support on our journey with Christ, leaning on each other to grow as a community.

Although seemingly unrelated, social media is also about relationships. Through Twitter, Facebook and the like, people strengthen their relationships with friends and family and form relationships with people that they might never have the chance to meet personally, by sharing things that are important to them. Through social media, people gain a deeper understanding of and appreciation for their friends, their interests, their feelings and their thoughts. These relationships are so important to them that they are constantly updating their status, checking their messages, and looking for new, interesting thoughts to share with their friends and followers.

This kind of understanding has long been a crucial aspect of the Church. It is through friendships that people have earned the right to witness to non-believers and grow in their faith through their friendships within the Church. Take a moment to consider the verbiage of Twitter relationships: they call each other "followers". We have long been followers of Christ through relationships that were formed thousands of years before we ever came into this world.

Social media essentially works in the same manner that early Christianity did. One person shares a message with their group of friends and followers, who in turn share a message with their group of friends and followers, until eventually the message spreads to the world. Jesus shared His message with his small circle of 12 apostles, who took that message into the world and shared the Word with everyone they knew, who shared the Word with everyone they knew, until eventually, 2,000 years later, that message was passed through the world and through the ages to us.

We all have our "turning point" moment with Christianity and mine came during my *Walk to Emmaus*, a retreat weekend focused on experiencing the Grace of God (for more information see www.upperroom.org). During my Emmaus weekend, we learned about what Christian discipleship truly means, how the Body of Christ comes alive in the community, and how to bring it to others. Many of us are not doing everything we can to bring Christ to others and to be a guiding hand toward the Emmaus moments of others. Many Christians are intimidated by the idea of evangelizing; they do not feel that they have the self assurance or proper tools to reach others in an effective non-confronting way. Our congregation members feel poorly prepared to go out into the world and evangelize. Social media provides Christians a means of incorporating evangelism into their daily lives through social networking.

When we think of Emmaus, we must recall the story behind it, as the risen Christ came upon two mourning disciples, too caught up in their grief and their troubles to see the big picture and the greater purpose. Many have compared this near-sighted view to the Church today, too caught up with the daily troubles of the Church, planning activities, printing flyers, and dealing with other trivialities, that they fail to focus on the big picture. We have been put on this Earth to evangelize and to fulfill the Great Commission.

From the explosive growth of Facebook, it is evident that relationships are a crucial part of people's lives; since launching in 2004, Facebook has garnered over 500 billion users worldwide, or 1 out of every 13 people on Earth. People desperately need relationships and by inspiring them with the Word of God, He can impart to them how important a relationship with Jesus Christ is in their lives, far more important than any friend on Facebook or follower on Twitter, Christ is the relationship that gives their life purpose and meaning.

Let us now go into the world, form relationships, strengthen relationships, evangelize, and grow as a Christian community through God's gift of technology. Through social media, the wave that Jesus Christ started over 2,000 years ago will gain unprecedented momentum, travelling through the world at the lightning fast speed of the Information Era.

Sources

Brown, Rev. Craig S. *Shepherd of the Hills United Methodist Church.* October 24, 2006.

Burbary, Ken. "Facebook Demographics Revisited—2011 Statistics." *Web Business by Ken Burbary* March 7, 2011.

Chan, Francis. *Crazy Love: Overwhelmed by a Relentless God.* Colorado Springs: David C. Cook, 2008.

"Churches Embracing Social Media". *Social Media World* July 6, 2009.

Dodd, Brian. "What Churches Should Learn from Social Media and the Egyptian Revolution". *Brian Dodd on Leadership: helping Create a Soundtrack to the Lives of Leaders* January 29, 2011.

Glanfield, Tim. "Britain Second to France in Fertility Rate as Population Keep Growing." *The Times* August 28, 2009.

Global Mobile Statistics 2011." *mobiThinking* June 2011.

Godin, Seth. *Permission Marketing: Turning Strangers Into Friends and Friends Into Customers.* New York: Simon and Schuster, 1999.

Green, Lauren. "Christianity in China." FoxNews.com January 20, 2011.

Hartford Institute for Religion Research. "Fast Facts."

Kunerth, Jeff. "Catholic Church Embraces Social Media—With Limits". *Orland Sentinel* March 11, 2010.

Lavrusik, Vadim. "How Users in Egypt are Bypassing Twitter & Facebook Blocks." *Mashable* January 27, 2011.

McLaughlin, Craig. "Daily Scripture Meditations: Community". *Pastor's Blog* March 6, 2009.

Media Outreach. "The World is Shrinking!" Friday, March 25, 2011.

Penner, Glenn. *Is the Blood of the Martyrs **Really** the Seed of the Church?*

Platt, David. *Radical: Taking Back Your Faith from the American Dream.* Colorado Springs: Multnomah Books, 2010.

---*Radical Together: Unleashing the People of God for the Purpose of God.* Colorado Springs: Multnomah Books, 2011.

Pray, Adam. "Ministry at Melti."

Rainer, Thom S. *Breakout Churches: Discover How to Make the Leap.* Grand Rapids: Zondervan, 2005.

--- *Surprising Insights from the Unchurched and Proven Ways to Reach Them.* Grand Rapids: Zondervan, 2001.

Rainer, Thom and Sam Rainer. *Essential Church?: Reclaiming a Generation of Dropouts.* Nashville: B & H Publishing Group, 2008.

Rosman, Katherine. "Eat Your Vegetables, and Don't Forget to Tweet. *The Wall Street Journal.* Thursday, June 16, 2011.

Smietana, Bob. *The Tennessean.* November 7 2010.

Stetzer, Ed, Richie Stanley, and Jason Hayes. *Lost and Found: The Younger Unchurched and the Churches that Reach Them.* Nashville: B & H Publishing Group, 2009.

Sweet, Leonard. *The Gospel According to Starbucks: Living with a Grande Passion.* Colorado Springs: Waterbrook Multnomah Press, 2007.

Thomas, Amanda. "Churches Extending their Reach through Social Media." *Times-Georgian.* June 19 2011.

Warren, Rick. *The Purpose-Driven Life.* Grand Rapids: Zondervan, 2002.

---*The Mark of Maturity.* June 16, 2011.

Image Credits

Big Red Church and Wesley United Methodist Church. Facebook screenshots, "Join Us on Facebook" image.

Christ United Methodist Church Tulsa. "Serve the Master Golf Tournament" photos, "Stained Glass Windows" photos, and Profile Pictures.

Church at BattleCreek, The. Blog screenshots.

Facebook, Facebook Logo.

Foursquare, Foursquare Logo.

Google Places. Google Places Screenshot

Lord, Dr. Jason. "Crisis-Opportunity".

Persing, Brea. "A Heart 4 Italia." Blog screenshot.

Platt, David. Twitter screenshots.

Rainer, Thom. Twitter screenshots.

Twitter, Twitter Logo (multiple variations).

Warren, Rick. Twitter screenshots.

Yelp!, Yelp! Logo,Church Reviews from Las Vegas

YouTube, YouTube Logo.

Youth Ministry Today. Twitter screenshot.

www.ingramcontent.com/pod-product-compliance
Lightning Source LLC
LaVergne TN
LVHW042336060326
832902LV00006B/198